LEGENDS of FAITH

MISSIONARIES for Christ

Marilyn Boyer

First printing: October 2025

Master Books, P.O. Box 726, Green Forest, AR 72638

Master Books® is a division of the New Leaf Publishing Group, LLC.

ISBN: 978-1-68344-402-2
ISBN: 978-1-61458-955-6 (digital)
Library of Congress Control Number: 2025947733

Please consider requesting that a copy of this volume be purchased by your local library system.

Printed in the United States of America

Visit our website for other great titles: www.masterbooks.com

For information regarding promotional opportunities, please contact the publicity department at pr@nlpg.com.

Table of Contents

Image Credits

Images created using Shutterstock AI.

Maps are from Shutterstock.com.

Introduction

In the pages of this book, you will meet men and women who lived lives totally dedicated to the service of their Savior, Jesus Christ. You will hear how they first became Christians and what inspired them to embark on their various missions. They had a burden to share the gospel with those living in remote areas who had not been exposed to the truth of God's Word. These missionaries, upheld by their tremendous faith in the Lord's providence, experienced much hardship and personal sacrifice. They all witnessed God at work in the saving of souls, but life was not easy for any of them. They relied on prayer and God's provision.

It was hard to choose which missionaries to write about, but I tried to give a glimpse into those involved in many different time periods and fields of service. Join me as we explore the adventurous lives of these servants of God.

- Adoniram Judson was one of the first Protestant missionaries sent from North America to the land of Burma. Here, he labored for 40 years. When Judson died, 100 Burmese churches had been started, with more than 8,000 believers.
- Robert Moffat was the first to translate and have the Bible printed in the Sechuana language. Besides faithfully preaching the gospel to the superstitious natives, he taught thousands of them how to read and write. Moffat spent 54 years of his life ministering in Africa.

- John Paton, who ministered in the South Seas, proclaimed in his autobiography that his ministry was undergirded by this thought: “This is strength; — this is peace: — to feel, in entering on every day, that all its duties and trial have been committed to the Lord Jesus, — that, come what may, He will use us for His glory and our own real good!”
- Hudson Taylor spent 54 years in China, laboring for five years before seeing his first convert to Christianity. He started China Inland Mission, which resulted in 20,000 Chinese people giving their lives to Christ.
- Amy Carmichael, missionary to India, learned that God makes no mistakes, even down to planning the color of your eyes. She opened an orphanage and rescued many children, becoming like a mother to them.
- Gladys Aylward worked as a housemaid until she saved enough money to pay her own fare to China. She constantly faced almost impossible circumstances, but she persevered and poured her heart into serving the Chinese people. She risked her life many times to help those in need and won the respect of the people of China.
- Eric Liddell was the first Scotsman ever to win an Olympic gold medal. As he explained to his fans, God called him to a more significant race — one where God gives out the medals. He committed his life to being a missionary to China. Having been raised in China by missionary parents, he had determined to one day return to share the gospel of his Lord Jesus Christ. He poured out his life for them and died as a prisoner of the Japanese during World War II.

- Betty Greene was the first woman missionary pilot and was one of the founders of Mission Aviation Fellowship. Hers was a life full of adventure poured out for the gospel.
- Jim Elliot, slain by the Auca Indians he shared the gospel with, embodied the importance of focusing on eternity and the faith. That is how he lived, and his testimony has inspired countless thousands to dedicate their lives to the Lord.
- Brother Andrew was a Dutch missionary who used his desire for adventure and his fearless nature to smuggle Bibles into Communist countries. He risked his life on countless occasions to bring the saving hope of the gospel to persecuted peoples. His ministry, Open Doors, continues today to deliver the message of salvation to oppressed people.

Remember that the whole world is a mission field. You don't have to go overseas to carry the gospel. It may be your neighbor that needs to hear the good news. God wants your life to honor Him wherever you live and whatever opportunities you pursue.

It is my hope that you will be inspired to rely on God to uphold you when life gets hard to bear. I pray that you will want to live a life dedicated to Christ. Learn to view life as from the loving Father's hand even when things grow difficult. Pray to the Lord to make your life one that is useful to the spread of the gospel of Jesus Christ. Remember the words of Isaiah 55:8-9, "For my thoughts are not your thoughts, neither are your ways my ways, saith the LORD. For as the heavens are higher than the earth, so are my ways higher than your ways, and my thoughts than your thoughts". As you meditate on the Word of God and hide it in your heart, ask Him to help you exchange your thoughts for His thoughts.

Always remember that God has the big picture in mind. We see only a tiny piece of the whole puzzle of eternity. Let the words of Romans 8:28 comfort you as you encounter the struggles of life: "And we know that all things work together for good to them that love God, to them who are the called according to his purpose." Isn't heaven going to be wonderful? We will get to personally meet these missionaries, and all the puzzling questions of life on earth will be answered there as we worship our great Lord and Savior.

1

Adoniram Judson

America's First Overseas Missionary

D. 1500 1550 1600 1650 1700 1750 **1788–1850** 1900 1950

"Yet when Christ calls me home, I shall go with the gladness of a boy bounding away from his school."[1]

Malden, Massachusetts – Born in 1788 , the son of a congregational minister.

Providence, Rhode Island – Took up deism after meeting Jacob Eames, a devoted deist.

Andover, Massachusetts – In 1808, Adoniram studied at Andover Seminary.

India; Burma – Unable to work in India, he went to serve Burma. He translated the gospel, completing the Burmese Bible. He was buried at sea in 1850, having died on a ship.

Who Was Adoniram Judson?

Although he was only 25 years old, Adoniram Judson was one of the first Protestant missionaries sent from North America to the land of Burma. Here, he labored for 40 years. During that time, he translated the Bible into the Burmese language. Judson's translation is still the most popular version used today. He also began compiling a Burmese-English dictionary. Every dictionary written since then has used Judson's original translation as a base. When Judson died in 1850, 100 Burmese churches had been started, with more than 8,000 believers. His ministry was the **impetus** for the first Baptist organization in America to support missionaries.

impetus: driving force

excelled: did extremely well

Early Years

Adoniram Judson was born on August 9, 1788, in Malden, Massachusetts. His father was a Congregational minister. Adoniram learned to read when he was three years old. Adoniram **excelled** in school. When he was 14, his father was offered the pastorate of the

Third Congregational Church of Plymouth, Massachusetts. This job change necessitated a family move from Braintree to Plymouth. The family built a lovely house overlooking the sea. A few months after moving, Adoniram became very sick. It took a year for him to fully recover. However, when he was better, he diligently pursued his studies and not only made up the work he missed, but also completed the next grade level. He was now ready for college. Six days after his 16th birthday, Adoniram left for Rhode Island College at Providence (soon to become Brown University), 50 miles from home.

freshman: first-year student

sophomore: second-year student

valedictorian: highest achiever

College Years

Adoniram took the entrance exams and, much to his amazement, scored so well that he skipped his **freshman** year and entered as a **sophomore**. Although Adoniram excelled at his studies, he began to develop friendships with a couple of boys who were a bad influence on his character. Jacob Eames, his best friend, was a devoted deist. As such, he believed that God existed but had little interest in the lives of people. He did not believe that Jesus was the Son of God. Deism appealed to Adoniram. His strong friendship with Jacob led to his abandoning the faith he had been taught as a boy, although he never mentioned that to his father. In three years, Adoniram graduated as **valedictorian** of his class.

Adoniram Leaves Home

When he returned home, Adoniram opened a small school for girls in his hometown. Unsatisfied with the quality of textbooks available

alma mater: university attended

unscrupulous: lacking morals

to his students, he wrote two textbooks: *Elements of English Grammar* and *The Young Lady's Arithmetic*. He got them published with the backing of his **alma mater**, Brown University. The school was successful, but Adoniram became bored with life. Because he was living at home again, his father expected him to participate in daily Bible reading and prayer. When he was 20, he told his parents he had been a deist for the last three years. Shocked, his parents tried to reason with him but could not persuade him to change his mind. They resorted to prayer.

Adoniram announced that he planned to leave his successful teaching career and go to New York. He and Jacob had dreamed about joining the theater. Although he had lost touch with Jacob, he believed New York would be a good place to try his hand at the theater. The young theater students he associated with there were mainly uneducated and **unscrupulous**. Since they had no money, they would seek lodging at night and then sneak away in the morning without paying the bill. Having no savings, Adoniram adopted this practice for a month but felt very guilty about it. He often wondered what his friend Jacob Eames was doing. He supposed Jacob was living a successful life by now.

Adoniram decided that theater was not for him. He set off on his horse and headed westward. Stopping at an inn for the night, he ended up in a room next to a dying man. Throughout the night, he tried to sleep despite the groans of pain coming from the adjoining

room. Unable to sleep, he wondered if the man in the next room believed in life after death. Adoniram was plagued with thoughts about what would happen to him if he were to die. Around 4:00 a.m., the groaning stopped, and Adoniram dozed off. In the morning, the innkeeper told him that the person in the next room had died at 4:00 a.m. Inquiring about the man, Adoniram was stunned to learn that the dying man was Jacob Eames, his college buddy. Jacob, who had been so sure there was no life after death where was he now? Had he been right?

seminary: school to train pastors

Adoniram Becomes a Christian

Adoniram was shaken to the core. He decided he would return home to Plymouth to try to sort out all these thoughts and doubts that tormented him. He explained his dilemma to his parents, who tried to help him learn the truth. About this time, two well-respected pastors came to stay with the Judsons. They wanted to discuss plans with Pastor Judson for opening a **seminary** in Andover, Massachusetts. Adoniram bombarded them with his many questions about Christianity. Sensing his sincerity, they offered to enroll him in Andover — not as a future pastor, but as one who wanted to learn more about Christianity. On October 12, 1808, Adoniram entered Andover Seminary.

Life in the seminary was not what he expected at all. Students were expected to chop their firewood, draw water from the well, and help the cook. They milked the cows, tended the gardens, and worked in the hayfields. This way, the students' cost was kept at a minimum. Adoniram spent hours studying the Bible in the original languages. He spent his spare time talking with the professors. Finally, on December 2, 1808, he was convinced. The Bible was truly the Word of God, and Adoniram was ready to commit his life to the Lord Jesus. His parents were overjoyed when they heard the news.

During his final year at Andover, Adoniram dedicated his life to becoming a **missionary**. He had seen a pamphlet which described the condition of people in India. They were steeped in **superstition** and **idolatrous** practices. They believed that each person had many lives and how they lived in this present life would determine in what form they would return in the next life. Someone who lived badly might return as a rat or an ant. A person who lived a good life might return as a prince or princess. Somehow, Adoniram knew from this point on that God wanted him to share the gospel with these fearful, misled people.

missionary: one sent to spread the gospel overseas

superstition: a fear-driven false belief

idolatrous: worship of false gods

America's First Missionary to India

Adoniram and three other like-minded students appeared before the Congregationalists' General Association in 1810 to appeal for support. On September 19, he was chosen to be a missionary to India and **commissioned** by the Congregational Church. After the meeting, he was invited to dinner at one of the deacon's homes. Here, he met and fell in love with Ann Hasseltine, one of the deacon's five children. After seeing each other for a month, Adoniram asked Ann to marry him, and she accepted. The couple was married on February 5, 1812. On February 19, Adoniram and Ann set sail for Calcutta, India. Adoniram used the long hours on the voyage to study the Bible. They arrived on June 17.

commissioned: chosen for a specific task

monopoly: exclusive control

Unwanted in India

Upon arrival in India, all newcomers were expected to register at the local police station. The East India Tea Company was a British trading company. It had a **monopoly** on imported tea from Asia, which it then sold in Britain and the colonies. The company had

lobbying: trying to influence

evangelizing: sharing the gospel

significant **lobbying** power in Parliament. The East India Tea Company opposed the Americans **evangelizing** the Hindu people. The police recorded the arrival of the missionaries but told them the decision of whether they were permitted to stay or forced to leave would be left to the East India Tea Company.

While waiting to hear, Adoniram visited William Carey, a famous missionary who had founded the Baptist Missionary Society. He was known as the "Father of Modern Missions." He was employed by Fort William College as a professor of oriental Languages. He also supported a large missionary community at Semaphore, located farther up the Hooghly River. Carey explained to Judson that the country of Burma was in great need of the gospel. It was home to 15 million people, and not one Bible was available in their language. Carey had much to say about Burma, but he was not encouraging about the possibility of the missionaries being allowed to stay in India.

Carey invited Adoniram and Ann to stay at Semaphore until permission to remain in India was granted or denied. He showed them the printing press he had set up. His print shop had recently been **ravaged** by a fire, and all of Carey's years of complicated translation work had been lost. **Undeterred**, he was producing the translations again. The East India Tea Company, which controlled much of India at the time, had a policy that prohibited Christian missionaries from settling in India. Eventually, they told the Judsons they would have to leave India voluntarily or be deported to England.

ravaged: destroyed

undeterred: persevering through setbacks

dilapidated: neglected, run-down

en route: on the way

Providentially, Adoniram found a rather **dilapidated** ship headed for Rangoon, Burma. The East India Tea Company traded in Burma, but Adoniram knew of no policy excluding mission work there. He and Ann felt that God had provided this option for them, and they decided to head for Burma, trusting the Lord to work out the details. William Carey had told them that his son Felix lived in Rangoon. Perhaps he could help them. The ship met with stormy weather **en route,** and sadly, Ann miscarried their first child before arriving in Rangoon.

Learning the Language

Arriving at the home of Felix Carey, William's son, Adoniram and Ann were warmly welcomed. Felix lived in a solidly built home, unlike the impoverished bamboo huts inhabited by the Burmese. The Careys were just about to embark on a visit to Semaphore to spend time with Felix's father. He was happy to offer the Judsons the house if they promised to care for it while he and his family were gone. He also left his servants to help them — a housekeeper, a cook, and a boy to care for the yard. Felix introduced them to a

Hindu man who could teach them the Burmese language. They began language lessons, which lasted for 12 hours a day, six days a week. It was very frustrating to learn, especially because the tutor knew no English. Thankfully, Felix had left a book he had begun writing, which explained Burmese grammar. This was a great help to the Judsons in their studies. The couple longed to begin missionary work but knew they must first learn the language, so they applied their energies diligently.

Meeting the Officials

In October 1813, Adoniram met with Mya-day-men, the **viceroy** of Rangoon. Ann made a favorable impression on the vicereine, the ruler's wife. She invited Ann to visit any time. She said she was as fond of Ann as if she were her sister. In 1814, Felix and his family returned, but not to stay. Felix informed the Judsons that he had accepted a position in the Royal government in Ava, which required him to move away. The house was theirs to use. The Judsons were now the only official missionaries in Burma.

In May 1814, a society was founded in America which offered to support the Judsons in their work. They also received a message that George Hough, a printer who owned a printing press, was on his way to assist them. On September 11, 1814, another child was born to the Judsons — Roger Williams Judson, named after the missionary to the Native American people in New England. By that time, Ann could speak the language fluently, and Adoniram had almost finished the Burmese grammar book that Felix Carey had begun to write. When he completed the grammar book, he translated the Gospel of Matthew into Burmese. Finally, the Judsons had

viceroy: ruler in charge

learned enough to communicate with the local Burmese people.

zayat: a Burmese building

Adoniram began holding nightly meetings for the Burmese men, and Ann operated a school for Burmese girls. They produced a seven-page tract explaining the gospel in a unique way that the Burmese people could understand. George Hough printed 1,000 copies in early 1817. Burmese people would stop by the mission house and request a copy of "The Holy Book," their name for the tract.

The First Convert

Adoniram decided it might help to build a **zayat** to be used on Pagoda Street, the main street in town. This familiar type of building might help the Burmese to feel more comfortable attending meetings. Construction was completed in April 1819. Adoniram would sit on the steps every day, answering any questions the Burmese people had. He would call out to passers-by, "Ho, everyone who thirsts for knowledge, enter here."[2]

Ann, in a letter to her father, wrote, "On the last day of April, a poor man came to the zayat. He is about 35 years old. His name is Maung Nau. He was very attentive, and he came back to our Sunday service. The next day and the next, he spent hours talking to Adoniram. At a meeting on May 5th, it seemed he was near to becoming a Christian ... and the following Sunday, he professed faith in Jesus!! Maung Nau is our very first convert. Papa, after nearly six years in Burma, we have a convert and that makes it all worthwhile!"[3]

The Ministry Grows

Slowly, other Burmese people came to know the Lord. By 1823, ten years after Adoniram's arrival, the church membership had grown to 18. Judson had completed **translating** the New Testament into the Burmese language.

Trouble began to brew between Britain and Burma. Britain desired more trade, and the Burmese desired more land holdings. Britain attacked and captured two Burmese provinces, which extended her trade routes to Eastern Asia. With the onset of the Anglo-Burmese war from 1824 to 1826, English-speaking Americans were mistaken for spies. Judson was imprisoned and treated cruelly for 20 months. Ann often visited Adoniram. She sewed his translation of the Bible into a pillow and brought it to him in prison. She tried many times to **procure** his release. Ann gave birth to their third child while Adoniram was imprisoned. Ann visited him with baby Maria and two little Burmese girls she was caring for.

translating: changing one language into another

procure: to secure

Finally, the British won the war. They released Adoniram and, to his surprise, asked for his assistance in drawing up the peace treaty because he understood the language and they did not. Taking his family with him, he began translating the Treaty of Yandabo. When he finished the treaty translation in March 1826, the Judsons returned to Rangoon. They found their house in disrepair from the war, but fixable. Maung Ing, a faithful convert, had found the pillow the prison guards had disposed of and kept it safe. It contained the precious translation of the Scriptures, Adoniram's work of nine years. Adoniram was overjoyed that his work had not been lost. They found their converts safe and growing in faith.

More Translation

The East India Company then called on Adoniram to help translate and write a contract with the Burmese government regarding imports and exports to and from the country. In exchange for his help, they agreed to persuade the Burmese government to allow religious freedom for the Burmese people. This would allow them to become Christians without fear of punishment or death. Although Adoniram did not want to leave his family again, he realized this government action would be crucial to the spread of the gospel. Sadly, before he finished the translation, he received a letter saying, "To sum up the unhappy tidings in a few words — Mrs. Judson is no more."[4] Adoniram was heartbroken. His dear, faithful wife and best friend in all the world had developed a severe fever and died suddenly.

To help relieve his grief, Judson threw himself into the work at hand. The Baptist Mission Society in the United States was sending more missionaries his way. George and Sarah Boardman arrived with their baby daughter. Six months after Ann's death, two-year-old Maria also died. Although greatly saddened by his losses, Adoniram saw encouragement in the ministry. In March, he attended a festival where he distributed 10,000 tracts. As a result, 6,000 people came to the mission house with questions about what they had read. It had taken him nine years to win the first 18 converts, but with the new religious freedom after the war, 217 Burmese people were saved.

Sarah

Adoniram spent the next two and a half years doing translation work six days a week. On January 31, 1834, he finished the translation. He received a letter of congratulations from Sarah Boardman. She informed him that George had died three years before. Sarah had remained to carry on their ministry. The two continued corresponding, and on April 1, 1834, they were married. Sarah had a passion for translation as well. She was working on translating gospel literature into Taling, one of the tribal languages spoken in Burma. Adoniram was busy teaching classes to his church of 100 members.

In October 1840, 27 years after he and Ann had arrived in Burma, the 1,200-page Burmese Bible was printed and ready for distribution. All his painstaking work had paid off. Finally, the Burmese people could read the Bible in their own language.

In March of 1850, Judson developed a serious lung disease. His doctor suggested a sea voyage might help him regain strength. When asked if he was prepared to die, he replied, "I am not tired of my work; neither am I tired of the world. Yet when Christ calls me home, I shall go with the gladness of a boy bounding away from his school."[5] Judson left on April 3, bound for the Isle of France. Nine

days later, on April 12, 1850, Adoniram died on board the ship, not far from the coast of Burma. He was buried at sea. At the time he died, Burma had 100 churches and more than 8,000 believers. The Burmese Bible he worked so hard to translate remains the most popular Burmese Bible in use today. Every Burmese dictionary and grammar book written since 1850 has been based on the original ones Adoniram wrote. A memorial was built in Plymouth, Massachusetts, honoring Adoniram Judson, America's first overseas missionary.

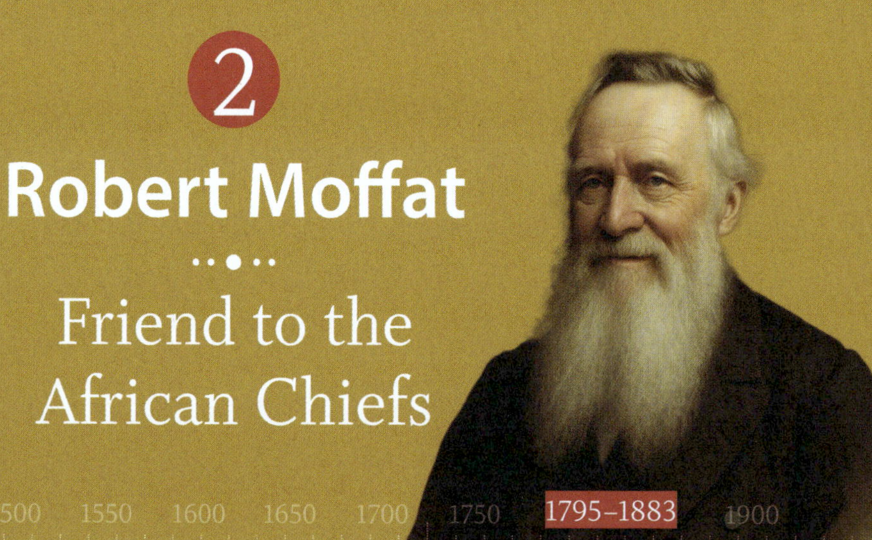

2

Robert Moffat

Friend to the African Chiefs

"... how amazing it is that Jesus came from His home in heaven to earth to show us what God is like and that He loves us."[6]

Ormiston, Scotland – Born in 1795, the son of a customs officer.

Manchester, England – After a crisis of faith, he was determined to become a missionary.

Cape Town, Africa – Robert studies the Dutch language and begins a journey to meet a native chief named Afrikaner and his people.

Lattakoo, South Africa – He translates the Bible and other books into the Sechuana language, serving in Africa for over 50 years and dying at age 87.

Who Was Robert Moffat?

Robert Moffat was a Scottish Congregational missionary who carried the gospel **predominantly** to the southern region of the continent of Africa. Moffat was the first to translate and have the Bible printed in the Sechuana language. Besides faithfully preaching the gospel to the superstitious natives, he taught thousands of them how to read and write. Moffat spent 54 years of his life ministering in Africa.

Early Years

Robert Moffat was born in Ormiston, Scotland, on December 21, 1795. His father was a customs officer whose job was to ensure no **contraband** came into the country and that all taxes were properly paid. Robert spent his boyhood years exploring the busy village and hiking the clifftop that overlooked the small bay. Evenings were spent around the fire with his God-fearing family. He learned with his brothers and sisters to sew and patch their clothes because money was scarce; nothing could be wasted. This skill was a blessing to him later in life. The family could not afford many books, but they owned a Bible, which they read daily. Robert's parents also had a catechism book from which they taught doctrine to the children on Sunday afternoons. The Moffats revered the Bible as the most significant book in the entire world.

Robert had an adventurous spirit and spent much time at the docks, helping the sailors. This prepared him to engage people in friendly conversation. He attended school for only a short time. When he was 11, Robert was **apprenticed**

predominantly: mostly

contraband: illegal items

apprenticed: learned a trade

as a gardener. He had to work hard 12 hours a day, six days a week, rising at 4:00 a.m. At 17, he left Scotland to become a gardener at an estate at High Leigh in Cheshire, England. Before Robert departed, his mother made him promise that he would read a chapter of the Bible each morning and each evening. He always kept that promise.

Moving to England

Robert's ship arrived safely at Liverpool. From there, he had to walk 27 miles to High Leigh. He enjoyed gardening, and as a bonus, his employer allowed him to read books from his sizable personal library. Robert spent many spare hours reading. During his time at High Leigh, Robert started attending the Methodist chapel. He began to question his salvation. It seriously concerned him. He spent much time studying the Bible and praying about it. One night while reading the Word, he acknowledged to God that he was a sinner and asked Jesus to be Lord of his life. That was the turning point. Robert knew for sure he would go to heaven when he died. He told his parents about his newfound faith, and they were thrilled. He began to volunteer in the Methodist chapel and became more confident in his faith.

While walking in town one day, Robert noticed an outdated sign announcing a missionary meeting that had already taken place. He remembered stories his mother had read to the family about Moravian missionaries in Greenland. His spirit was stirred, and he determined he would become a missionary!

Soon afterward, he attended a Methodist conference in Manchester, England. A man named Mr. Roby conducted the conference. Robert told him about his desire, and Mr. Roby promised to write a letter to the London Missionary Society, recommending Robert to them. He also secured a job for Robert as a gardener at the home of Mr. James Smith. Mr. Smith was a gardener with a great passion for mission work. Robert worked diligently and studied under Mr. Roby in his spare time. He eventually fell in love with Mr. Smith's daughter Mary, whom he married several years later. After Robert had studied under Mr. Roby for a year, the London Missionary Society sent him to the mission fields of Africa.

Off to Africa

One October morning in 1816, Robert Moffat's parents bade him goodbye, and he left on the ship *Alacrity*, bound for Cape Town,

Africa. Three months later, he arrived. As he stood on deck and gazed at the land he had dreamed of for so long, he threw his head back and laughed. "What fun! What tremendous fun!" he shouted.[7]

kraal: houses surrounding a livestock pen

porters: people who carry others' cargo

arduous: very difficult

While awaiting his specific assignment from the mission, Robert began to learn the Dutch language. The Mission Society leaders sent him to work in the **kraal** of a native chief named Afrikaner. They told him this chief was known to be cruel and unpredictable; not only that, but his destination was remote and would require months of travel to get there.

Robert began preparations. He gathered pack animals — some to help him carry supplies and some to use for food once he arrived. He needed gardening tools and seeds. Once he was ready, he started out in a covered wagon drawn by 16 or 18 oxen. A wagon driver and a group of **porters** accompanied him on the journey. They traveled on dust-covered, jagged paths. It was slow and **arduous**.

Dutch-speaking settlers from the Netherlands, called Boers, lived in the area where Robert was traveling. Local natives worked for the Boers as servants and knew the Dutch language. This made it easier for Robert to communicate with them all. Boer homesteads were isolated. Robert was welcomed to rest at one of them by a farmer who read the Bible to his family regularly. He was excited to have a missionary in his home. He asked Robert to lead his family in a proper Bible service that evening. His wife prepared the best meal Robert had tasted in months.

Arriving at Namaqualand

Robert and his companions still had many miles to go, and there were many challenges. Farmers along the way told stories about Afrikaner. They were concerned that Robert might be killed by this violent man. Travel became more and more challenging. The rough roads turned to sand, making it **cumbersome** for the oxen to pull the wagon. The animals' feet burned as they plodded on the hot desert sands during the day. Water became extremely scarce. Eventually, they traveled at night when it was cooler. Robert was fearful that if they did not find water soon, both oxen and people would die of thirst. He prayed desperately.

> **cumbersome:** difficult to move
>
> **pressed on:** forced themselves to continue
>
> **Namaqualand:** a South African desert

Finally, the oxen were too thirsty to go on. Robert's only hope was to dig deep in the sand. Perhaps they could find water. Amazingly, they did reach a small amount of water, enough for both men and beasts to drink. The food supply was running out, and the men were hungry, but they **pressed on** and reached their destination: **Namaqualand**. It had been four long, harsh months since he had left Cape Town.

Meeting Afrikaner

Robert immediately went to meet Afrikaner, the dreaded chief. Surprisingly, the chief, speaking Dutch, asked Robert if he was the true, official missionary. Then, the chief inquired how long Robert planned to stay. Robert replied he would be there indefinitely. Chief Afrikaner responded, "Then you must have a house."[8] He told some women to build Robert a house from branches and grass.

leisurely: slow

Before Robert arrived, another missionary, Mr. Ebner, had been working with the tribe, and the Lord had begun working in Afrikaner's heart. The chief had given up his murderous ways and wanted a missionary to teach his people. He proved to be a serious student of the Bible, although he was still learning Dutch. He had an exceptional memory and could recite anything that was read to him. Once, he exclaimed, "My head is too small. It is swelling with these great matters."[9] Robert began to teach at a more **leisurely** pace to give Afrikaner more time to understand the Scriptures.

Afrikaner and his people carefully watched how Robert responded to the many trials he faced. Robert had to cook his own food. If meat was not available, he would live for weeks on milk. Robert managed to meet each trial with cheerfulness and resolve. When he encountered the cruel practices of the natives, he tried to teach them gentler ways of doing things. For instance, when a person

became too old to work, the custom was to abandon him or her to die in the desert. Robert showed them a better way.

Each evening, Robert would play hymns on his violin and teach them to the people. He held a service in the morning and a service in the evening, and taught school to the children for three to four hours each day. He added hygiene to their school day — the people had never bathed before! He taught them how to wash their clothes as well. Afrikaner attended almost every service Robert held, listening carefully. Afrikaner repented for the evil he had done in the past. His people saw the change God made in his life.

At one point, Robert became deathly ill. Afrikaner sat by his bedside and read the New Testament to him until he recovered. One boy in the school noted, "The one who was like a lion is now more like a lamb."[10] The chief, whose first choice had always been fighting, was now instructing his people to learn the ways of God. Afrikaner had become a Christian. Robert Moffat was deeply thankful!

Helping Afrikaner and His People

Water was scarce in Afrikaner's kraal, making it almost impossible to grow food. Robert, an experienced gardener, urged Afrikaner to consider moving to another location before his people died of malnutrition. The problem was that Afrikaner had been so violent for so many years that people feared him. The governor had offered a reward for his capture. Afrikaner said no other tribes trusted him to live near them.

Robert came up with a plan. He told Afrikaner to disguise himself and pretend to be Robert's servant. Then they would go to Cape Town together and meet with the governor to explain that Afrikaner had become a Christian and now lived a peaceful life. On the way, they met farmers who were stunned when Robert told them of Afrikaner's conversion. The farmers were certainly eager to hear about the gospel that changed such a wicked person's life.

Lord Charles Somerset, the governor, observing the contrast in Afrikaner from his previous way of life, exclaimed to the chief, "It is a great pleasure to see the change in you. You are certainly not the man you were."[11] The governor did not arrest Afrikaner, but instead gave him a gift of a wagon in which to travel home. Afrikaner agreed that he should indeed move his people to a better land.

Robert Marries

A letter from Mary was awaiting Robert at Cape Town. It had taken a year to arrive. Her father had agreed to approve of her marriage to Robert. She planned to travel to Cape Town to meet him so they could get married there. It was December 1819 when Mary arrived by ship. They were married on January 20, 1820. Mary spent the next 50 years faithfully serving the native people with her husband.

Robert prepared three wagons to carry his new wife and her possessions to Lattakoo, the location chosen by the London Missionary Society for the couple to reside. The trip would take 66 days. The journey was **fraught** with danger. Water was scarce. When they finally reached Lattakoo, they found a church previously built by missionaries that could seat 400 people. Several attempts had been made to reach this tribe with the gospel, but little progress had been made before the Moffats arrived. Hardly any people attended the church. Near the church, there was a row of simple houses built for missionaries, with a garden spot for each one.

fraught: full

One day, Afrikaner arrived, bearing the goods Robert had left behind in his village. He told Robert he planned to move his people near the Moffats so they could continue learning about Jesus. Sadly, however, Afrikaner died shortly afterward. But Robert was thrilled with the report of Afrikaner's dying words. When he realized he was dying, the chief called for his family and his people to speak to the tribe. "We are not what we were — savages. We are people who say that we believe the gospel. Let us then live in peace with all men, if possible."[12] He also told them to stay together and to treat any missionaries who should come as ones sent from God. "I have great hope that God will bless you when I have gone to heaven. I feel that I love God. He had done so much for me, and I didn't deserve any of it."[13]

Learning the Language

Robert felt the need to learn the native language. Although the natives knew Dutch, they did not think in Dutch. He was concerned that the people were still lying and stealing. Besides that, he realized the interpreter was not always correct or accurate in translating Robert's teaching, and the people were confused. He set his mind to learning Sechuana. He was determined that one day, he would see the church filled with believers.

Robert suggested to Mary that he leave their home for a few months to live in the village with the people, learning to speak and write the language. Mary was always ready to support Robert's decisions, even if it meant additional hardship for her. By now, Mary had given birth to two daughters. The couple had rescued two children. Their mother had died, and according to tribal custom, the natives were about to bury them alive with their dead mother. Mary and Robert had willingly adopted them. Mary now had four children to care for. Although being very uneasy at the prospect of being alone with four children to care for without Robert there, she agreed. She trusted God for protection.

Robert traveled for six days to live with a young chief for ten weeks. He heard no Dutch or English, so he learned Sechuana the hard way. On his way to the village, he faced close calls with lions, but God protected him. His plan worked. Three months later when he returned to Mary, he could speak and understand the language almost as well as the natives.

Robert immediately began translating the Bible into Sechuana. He prayed for new opportunities to use the language. God answered that prayer: Robert spent the next 40 years ministering to the natives.

Robert wrote a spelling book for children and opened a school. Mary taught the women and girls how to sew. The Moffats had fabric sent to them to make their own clothes. The chief was amazed that the Moffats were giving their lives to help his people, even after his people had lied to them and stolen their things for so long. Robert used this to tell him, "You think it is amazing that we came from another country to live with you and tell you about the Lord Jesus. Then think how amazing it is that Jesus came from His home in heaven to earth to show us what God is like and that He loves us."[14] The natives nodded in agreement. They were beginning to understand. They also began to realize that they were sinners. They confessed that they had stolen from the missionaries and practiced cruelty toward others.

Ministering to the Ndebele Tribe

In May 1829, the school building was completed. That Sunday, many natives came to watch six of their friends stand and publicly confess that they believed in the Lord Jesus Christ. Robert and Mary now had ten children, as well as the native children they had rescued.

One day, messengers from a neighboring Ndebele tribe arrived peacefully. They had been sent by their chief to learn about the teachings of the white men, including the way they lived. They watched as the women sewed and wore clothes, something they had never seen before. They sat amazed at the church service, especially when the singing of hymns began.

They stayed for days and then insisted Robert accompany them home to meet their chief, the king. The messengers told the king about all the kindnesses shown to them by the Moffats. The king was known as one of the fiercest and most cruel of all the tribal chiefs. He laid his hand on Robert's shoulder and exclaimed, "My heart is white as milk. I am still wondering at the love of a stranger who never saw me. You have fed, you have protected me, and you have carried me in your arms. I live today, by you, a stranger."[15]

Robert did not understand. He asked when he had done these things for the king. The king explained that when he did these things for his two messengers, it was as if he did them for the king. Robert used this opportunity to share with the king how Jesus Christ had died on the Cross to save anyone who put their trust in Him. When Robert finally returned to Mary, the king sent warriors for protection and loaded the wagons with gifts. Robert had been gone for two months. Mary and all at the mission station were relieved that no harm had come to him.

Singing the ABCs

Robert taught the people how to grow many crops. He helped them plant fruit trees and nut trees. Soon, the people who had once been in danger of starvation were eating well. Robert spent many hours translating the Book of Luke so the people could read the Word themselves. Then he translated more of the New Testament. At first, he and Mary only taught the children to read, but the adults wanted to read as well. Robert taught them the letters by putting the alphabet to the music of an old Scottish song he had sung as a boy. Singing was heard in the village until the wee hours of the morning as the excited adults practiced the tune.

Back to England

The Moffats needed to return to England for a short time, mainly to print the New Testament Robert had translated. They spoke at many churches, telling stories about the Africans. People generously gave money to have Bibles published. Robert had 500 copies printed. The cold, damp English weather was tough on Robert's health. He had to take time to rest in bed. While resting, he began translating the Psalms into Sechuana. When he was nearly recovered, he spoke to young men studying to be missionaries. He met David Livingstone at one of the meetings and was impressed

with the young man. David attended all the meetings where Robert spoke, and on December 8, 1840, David boarded a ship bound for South Africa. He carried with him the 500 copies of the New Testament to distribute to the natives. When the Moffats returned to Cape Town, they met up with David. Robert had ordered 2,000 more New Testaments. David worked with the Moffats for a few years. He and Mary, the oldest Moffat daughter, fell in love and were married. They moved 250 miles from the Moffats to start a new ministry.

A Full Life of Ministry

Robert eventually translated the Old Testament as well. Several of their children became missionaries to Africa. As the couple grew old, the London Missionary Society decided that they should return to England. On Sunday, March 20, 1870, Robert preached his last sermon in Africa. He had ministered for more than 50 years by the time he returned to England.

wane: weaken

In England, Robert and Mary had many speaking opportunities. Unfortunately, Mary died of pneumonia less than a year after their return. Robert said, "For fifty-three years I have had her to pray for me. How lonely I feel."[16] However, he went back to work as a missionary speaker, intent on inspiring others to take up the challenge and commit to doing missions work.

Robert finished translating the Old Testament and got it off to the printer. He was still lecturing and speaking while in his 80s. Gradually, his strength began to **wane**. One night when he was 87 years old, he wound his watch before going to bed. "For the last time," he said, sensing the end was near.[17] He died peacefully during the night.

"In the Bible House in London, where Robert Moffat's Sechuana Bible was prepared for the press, is a memorial window to great translators of the Scriptures. Tyndale, Jerome, Luther, and Carey are there, and in their company stands Robert Moffat."[18] Robert once wrote, "It is a pleasing, sometimes an exciting exercise to look back on the rugged path which we have been called to tread and to recount the dangers from which a gracious Providence has rescued us. Some of these have been so striking that when I recall the circumstances, I am forcibly impressed with the sentiment that a man is immortal till his work is done."[19]

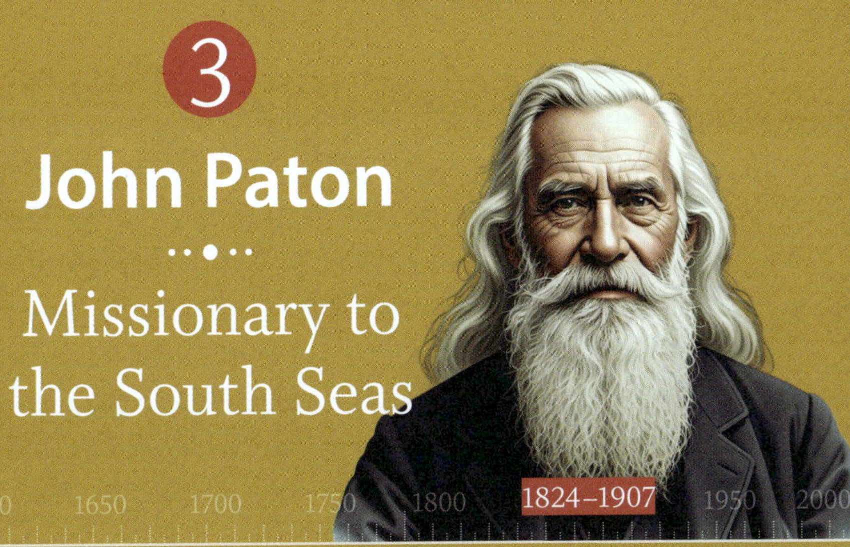

3

John Paton

Missionary to the South Seas

"God give me work while my life shall last, and life till my work be done."[20]

Braehead, Scotland – Born as the oldest of 11 children in 1824, grew up enjoying nature and reading the Bible; influenced by his father who prayed throughout the day.

Glasgow, Scotland – He was accepted to Normal Seminary in Glasgow. He finished college, divinity school, and medical school while also doing city mission work.

Tanna, New Hebrides – Soon after arrival, his wife and baby died. John stayed over three years, then death threats forced him to leave the island.

Aniwa, New Hebrides – John worked to teach the natives about digging wells, reading the Bible, and teaching Christian ways. He died at age 83.

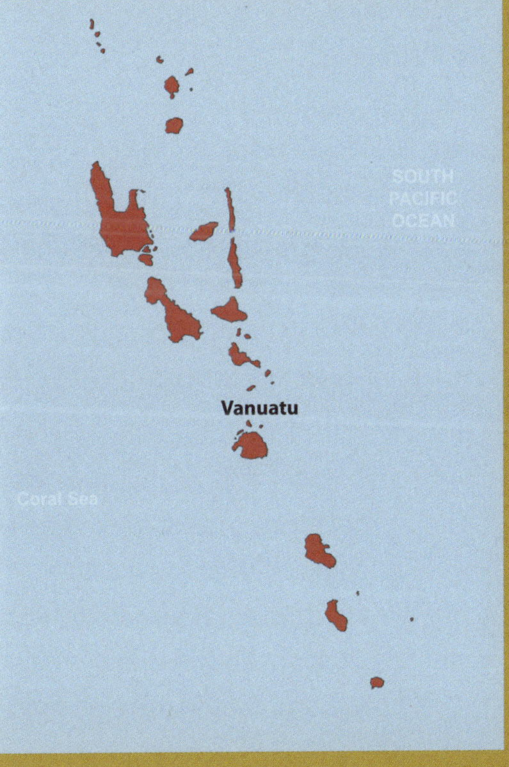

Who Was John Paton?

John Paton was a Scottish missionary to the New Hebrides islands in the South Pacific. Hearing of the need of these islands, he said he felt like responding to God's call as Isaiah did: "… Here am I. Send me" (Isaiah 6:8). Because the region was well known for its violence and extreme cruelty, many friends tried to dissuade him, but Paton's missionary resolve remained steadfast. He proclaimed that his ministry was guided by this thought: "This is strength; — this is peace: — to feel, in entering on every day, that all its duties and trials have been committed to the Lord Jesus, — that, come what may, He will use us for His glory and our own real good!"[21]

Early Days

John Paton was born on May 24, 1824, in Braehead, near Dumfries, Scotland. John was the oldest of the 11 children of his parents, James and Janet Paton. John had a happy childhood, exploring the woods and fields with his siblings. His parents loved God and faithfully read the Bible to the children and taught them to pray. His father had a "prayer closet," a room he entered daily after each meal to talk with God. The children would overhear his voice as he prayed for each one by name.

Once when his father was out of town longer than expected, the family ran out of food. John's mother gathered the children around and they all prayed for God to provide food. The next morning, a large package was delivered to their home. It contained a bag of new potatoes, flour, and some cheese. It was from their grandfather, who knew nothing of their need. Mrs. Paton gathered the children around to thank God in prayer. Then she told them,

martyrs: those who died for the faith

"O my children, love your heavenly Father, tell Him in faith and prayer all your needs, and He will supply your wants so far as it shall be for your good and His glory."[22]

On Sundays, the family attended church four miles away. Sunday afternoons were spent discussing the sermon, listening to their father tell Bible stories, stories of the **martyrs**, or reading from *Pilgrim's Progress*. Then their father asked them Bible questions about what they had studied. Whoever answered the most questions was rewarded by being chosen to read the Scripture aloud to the family. Finally, everyone spent time again praying.

John later wrote about how his father's prayers influenced him. "How much my father's prayers at this time impressed me, I can never explain, nor could any stranger understand. When, on his knees and all of us kneeling around him in Family Worship, he poured out his whole soul with tears for the conversion of the Heathen world to the service of Jesus, and for every personal and domestic need, we all felt as if in the presence of the living Savior, and learned to know and love him as our Divine friend."[23]

John went to the village school until he was 12 years old. He then helped his father in his workshop where they made stockings. He worked from 6:00 in the morning until 10:00 at night, with half an hour each for breakfast, lunch, and supper. John gave his life to the Lord when he was a teenager, alone in his room one night reading the Bible. He confessed his sin and asked Jesus to be his Lord and Savior. In his few spare moments after work each day, John began to study Latin and Greek. Inspired by the stories he had grown up hearing, he felt a deep desire to dedicate his life to becoming a missionary.

Moving to Glasgow

John felt he needed more education to prepare for being a missionary. He applied to the Normal Seminary in Glasgow, the capital of Scotland. He was accepted and heard of a job at the church there that would help pay for his tuition. The job **entailed** visiting absentees from the church and passing out gospel tracts. By taking the job, he would have the opportunity to receive a year's training at the Normal Seminary. He applied for the job and obtained it; two days later, he wrapped up his few clothes and his Bible and set out to walk 40 miles to catch a train for the rest of the journey. His father walked the first six miles with him, giving him good advice

entailed: included

along the way. Finally, they hugged, and Mr. Paton prayed for his son. As John hiked on, he kept looking back to see his beloved father still watching him go. John was deeply moved and vowed that with God's help, he would never do anything to grieve his dear parents.

John had to work part-time to pay for his education. His funds ran so low at one point that he considered quitting. Then he noticed a sign in a window advertising a teaching position. He applied, got the position, and continued with his studies. Although he struggled financially, he finished college, divinity school, and finally, medical school. Because he was the oldest child, he felt responsible for helping his siblings. God provided for his needs, and he even saved enough money to buy a cow for his family. He helped pay for his siblings' clothes and school fees.

Mission Work

John paid for his last 10 years of schooling by doing city missionary work for the Glasgow City Mission. He started out holding meetings in a hayloft, bringing in unbelievers and **drunkards**, with whom he shared the gospel. His meetings grew, and the mission bought buildings on Green Street for him. His mission then became known as the Green Street City Mission. He started schools for poor children, who began to realize if they learned to read and write, they might have opportunities to leave the industrial slums in which they lived.

John held Sunday morning Bible classes at 7:00 for over 100 of the city's poorest young men and women. He would start at 6:00 a.m., walking

drunkards: people addicted to strong drink

> **doctrine:** beliefs taught in the Bible
>
> **abstinence:** refraining from strong drink

from street to street, knocking on doors and inviting folks to church. He held a Wednesday evening prayer meeting, a Thursday evening meeting to teach **doctrine**, and a Friday evening singing class. On Saturday, he held a total **abstinence** class to encourage the people to give up drinking alcoholic beverages. He visited the homes of the sick and troubled. Often, he had little time for his own studies. Once, he visited a dying unbeliever who had been trying to discourage people from attending church. The man was close to death and asked how to be saved. Fortunately, he recovered and helped John with the ministry, influencing many to turn to Christ. Attendance at John's services grew to 600 people.

Missionary to the New Hebrides

At last, John completed his medical training. He told the Foreign Mission Committee that he was ready to go wherever they wanted to send him. They decided to send him to the South Pacific islands called the New Hebrides. Friends feared for his safety and advised him against going there. The natives were known to resort to very

cruel practices at times, in their worship of false gods. John lovingly responded to friends by saying, "I have only one time to die, and I am willing to leave the manner of it with God."[24]

His parents were happy with his decision to be a missionary. His father said, "Your mother and I were thrilled when you were born, our first child. We gave you to God, praying that He would call you to be a missionary. We decided not to tell you that before, as you needed to be certain for yourself."[25] "We pray with all our hearts that the Lord may long spare you and give you many souls from the heathen world."[26]

John had recently met Mary Ann Robson, a dedicated Christian woman. She shared his desire to become a missionary, and soon they were married. His parents were pleased that Mary would accompany their son to the mission field. John's brother Walter agreed to take over his ministry at Green Street Mission.

Preparations were underway just as soon as John and Mary were married. They had to plan carefully to be sure they would have all the supplies needed with them. Mary was able to bring along her piano to play music for the natives. They traveled to Australia by cargo ship. At Sydney, they boarded another ship **bound for** the New Hebrides islands. Mary was six months pregnant when they finally landed on Anatom, 10 miles from Tanna, their destination.

Dr. Geddie, a medical missionary, met them and offered to send some Christian natives with them to Tanna. One of those who accompanied them was a native who had changed his name to Abraham when he was converted. He proved to be a dear friend and helper. John purchased land at Tanna from the natives and began to build a house for Mary and

bound for: sailing to

himself to live in. He paid natives with fishhooks, blankets, and axes for their assistance.

The First Months on Tanna

At first, Mary and John were shocked by the natives of Tanna, who were very superstitious and had cruel practices. Nevertheless, both were convinced that God had called them to Tanna. Mary was determined to help the poor women. Soon she was holding classes to teach the women and young girls to sing and sew. John was determined to produce a written language for the people. When they had only been at Tanna for three months, a baby boy was born to them. Joy was turned into deep sadness when Mary became ill with pneumonia. Just before she died, she said, "Don't think I regret coming here. I would do it again, with all my heart. Not lost, gone before to be forever with the Lord."[27] After another three weeks passed, the baby died as well. John slept on the graves of his wife and baby son for many nights to keep the natives from disturbing the graves.

Not long after these tragedies, John came down with malaria. A friendly native chief from whom he had bought the land told him, "If you stay here, you will die soon. We never sleep so near a swamp as you do. We sleep on high ground, and the fresh wind keeps us well."[28] Abraham offered to help him relocate his house.

John was thankful for Abraham. He wrote, "How good dear Abraham is! How sincerely devoted to me and to Jesus! And he was once a wild heathen. What power is in the gospel. God, give me health and long life that I may teach the gospel to these people."[29] Abraham and his wife helped to nurse John back to health. When he was able to build another house, he seldom had malaria again.

John was making small inroads with the natives. They lied and stole many things from John, including his pots and pans, bed linens, and even chickens. Often, his life was threatened, but God protected him each time. Fear was a way of life for the natives. John wanted to rescue them from its grip. He continued to preach and teach the natives. One night, after traveling and preaching all day, he prayed, "O my gracious Father, have mercy on these poor people. I have seen so many whose lives are full of fears and terrors. Help them to remember and understand the things I taught them today about the true and loving God. I am thankful that the light is beginning to come to some of them. I love them. Though my life is often in danger here, I am willing to work among them. Make me strong in body and soul for Thee."[30]

John labored on Tanna for three and a half years. Whenever storms or sickness came, the superstitious natives blamed it on Paton's God. Often, a native would appear close to becoming a Christian but then fall back to the tribal ways. Many times, John's faithful dog Clutha was the one who alerted him to danger.

Some of the Tannese people conspired to kill him, but others pledged to stand by the "mission-man," as they called him. One morning, armed men surrounded his house, declaring they were there to kill him. John recognized a few of the men who had attended his church services recently. After kneeling in prayer, he arose and spoke to them, "Have I ever harmed you or have I tried to help you?"[31] Amazingly, the men began to wander away. John's life was again spared.

Recruiting in Australia

Word got to representatives from the Foreign Mission Board on nearby Aneityum that Paton's life was in danger. Being responsible for having sent the Patons to the South Seas, they sent a ship to rescue him and strongly suggested that John go to Australia. They explained to him, "You have gone through so many hard things that you are nearly broken in health. We think a visit to Australia would do you much good. Besides, we need more money and missionaries

for these islands. If you would go and speak to the churches, you could get much help for our mission."[32] They sent him with a letter of introduction to a minister there. He was in great demand and spoke at many churches and Sunday schools. Sunday school children raised enough money to purchase a mission ship to carry supplies and missionaries from one island to another. That ship could also be used to rescue any missionaries who might be in danger.

Now that the ship was paid for, John was sent to Scotland to recruit more people. He spent a few months speaking at churches and raising more money for the South Seas mission. He recruited four more missionaries while there. He also married Margaret Whitecross, who was dedicated to his mission. He visited his family before leaving; it was a sweet reunion.

Upon returning from Scotland, John and Margaret stayed in Australia; four years passed from the time John had left until he returned to Aneityum.

In November 1866, John, Margaret, and their first child were waiting for their assignment from the missionary society. They had not been told which island would be their destination. John told Margaret, "They are sure to send me back to Tanna. Nobody else knows the island at all and the islanders have had time to quiet down by now. As you know, I still want to help them more than anything else in the world, and my guess is that they would welcome us back now that they have been without help for a bit."[33] However, the missionary society felt it was still quite unsafe for white missionaries to settle in Tanna. John was very disappointed. Instead, he was sent to Aniwa, a small island near Tanna.

Life on Aniwa

John was now 43 years old. The Patons would serve for 15 years on Aniwa. The natives on this island were fierce and cruel like those on Tanna. John began building a new mission house, this time on high ground. He had to start all over learning to speak the Aniwanese language and studying their **vocabulary** to develop a written language. Over the years, John added a church, a school, an orphanage, a printing shop, a **joiner's** shop, and storehouses. It was almost a complete village when he was done.

> **vocabulary:** words used in communication
>
> **joiner's:** making wooden windows and doors

The greatest need for the island was a supply of fresh water. When John suggested they dig a well, the natives laughed, saying, "Who ever heard of water coming from beneath the ground?"[34] John worked day after day. Finally, he hit fresh water. The chief was reluctant to take a sip, but when he did, he was astounded. John later said that successfully digging that well did more for the cause of Christianity on Aniwa than years of teaching could have done! Namakei, the

chief, told his people, "No god of Aniwa's ever answered our prayers the way Missi's (their name for John) does. If He can bring rain up from the earth, as we have seen with our eyes, why then I believe also all the other things which Missi tells us."[35] From that day, the natives began attending church and school. Namakei and another chief, watching how Margaret cared for her baby, brought their little daughters and asked the missionaries to bring them up in Christian ways.

More Opportunities

labored: worked hard

Life for the natives was dangerous. Many children were left without parents due to storms, fighting, and disease. John opened an orphanage to care for the children. On one occasion, John wanted to send a message to Margaret to bring him some tools. He wrote what he needed on a piece of wood and sent a native to bring it to her. The man could hardly believe his eyes. He thought, "Can wood talk?" John explained what written language was and told him that he was in the process of writing a language for them. Eventually, they had Bibles printed and John taught them to read. He also got glasses for some who had trouble with their eyesight. Year by year, they **labored** as the little island drew closer to Christianity. One of the natives came to John, wanting a Christian wedding ceremony. The church was packed. The couple became good friends, and the husband was a trusted bodyguard to John.

Sundays were full days. The first service began at sunrise and lasted one hour. John held a special class for those interested in being baptized. After dinner was Sunday school. Then John traveled around the island, holding meetings at many villages. Evening

banyan: large fig
reap: benefit from

prayer was held under the **banyan** trees, where they sang hymns. At the mission house, orphans and villagers gathered to sing hymns and recite Bible verses. Though Sundays were busy and tiring, often, when John heard the converted cannibals praying, he would weep for joy. So, one little island in the South Pacific was won to Christianity.

Great Accomplishments

John wrote an autobiography at his brother's suggestion. It became a bestseller and was translated into many languages. He traveled to America, as well as to Scotland, Ireland, Australia, and Canada to raise funds. Aniwa was now Christianized.

John's heart was still with Tanna. He wanted to return. However, in 1896, the mission sent John's son Frank to Tanna as a missionary. John had the pleasure of helping his son and his young bride with the work he had begun years earlier. This time, Tanna was ready to accept the gospel. Soon, Frank began to **reap** the harvest sowed years ago by his father. John could hardly believe the difference

Frank made there in three years. At last, the natives of Tanna broke away from their heathen superstitions. John never gave up traveling to raise funds or recruit missionaries for the New Hebrides. When he was 80 years old, he went to the islands for the last time. He rejoiced that out of 30 islands, 25 now had established missions. After several weeks of illness, John died at the age of 83 on January 28, 1907. His prayer was answered. "God give me work while my life shall last, and life till my work be done."[36]

"... I cannot die because God had called me to China, and I have not been there yet."[37]

Barnsley, England – Born to Christian parents, as he got older, he could read the Bible in Latin and worked at a bank.

Hull, England – Hudson learned to work with and dispense medicines, and took classes at the medical school. He prepared to do mission work in China.

Shanghai, China – He learned the Chinese language, worked at a local hospital, started a church in Ning-po, and eventually contracted tuberculosis and returned to England.

Hang-Chow, China – He returned to China and opened a hospital and continued to grow the China Inland Mission. Hudson dies in 1905.

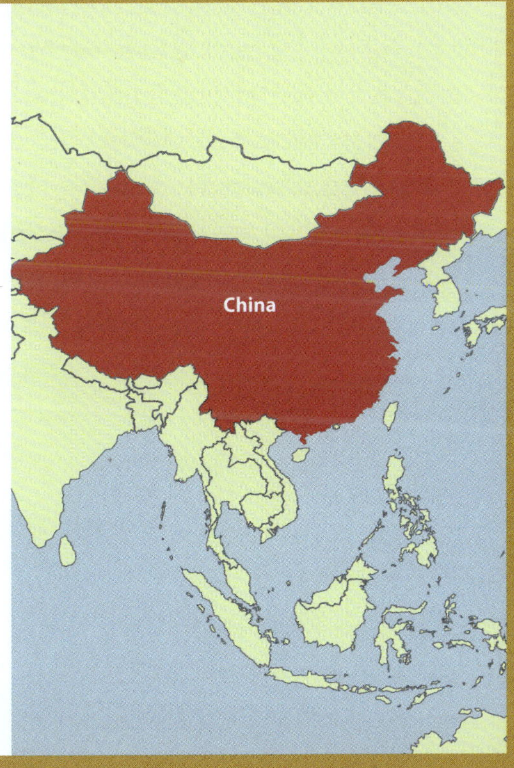

Who Was Hudson Taylor?

Hudson Taylor was a British missionary who dedicated his life to bringing the gospel to China. He spent 54 years in China, laboring for five years before seeing his first convert to Christianity. Taylor founded the China Inland Mission, which was responsible for bringing more than 800 missionaries to the country. The efforts of China Inland Mission resulted in 20,000 Chinese people giving their lives to Christ.

Hudson Taylor was born at Barnsley in Yorkshire, England, on May 21, 1832. His parents were Christians, and his father, a **pharmacist**, faithfully led his family each night in Bible reading and prayer. Partly because of that, Hudson had a wealth of Bible knowledge and could even read the Bible in Latin. As a young man, Hudson worked with his father in the pharmacy. The family attended church together each Sunday. Hudson had two younger sisters, Amelia and Louisa. He was particularly close to Amelia.

Hudson worked at Barnsley Bank for three years. There, he met young friends who planted seeds of doubt in his mind regarding Christianity. His sister Amelia noticed that he seemed to be drifting away from God. She committed to pray three times a day for his salvation. His mother was devoted to praying for him as well.

pharmacist: a dispenser of prescriptions

evangelistic: presentation of the Savior

Hudson Is Saved

One day, 17-year-old Hudson was feeling unusually bored. He picked up an **evangelistic** tract his father was distributing to customers. He headed for his favorite reading spot — an old warehouse at the back of their property. At the exact time Hudson was reading the tract, his mother was praying for his salvation. The first part of the tract had an exciting story, and the second part of the booklet was a gospel message. As Hudson read the familiar gospel message, some wording seemed to shout out at him: "The finished work of Christ."[38] God used that phrase to prick his conscience and there in the warehouse, he gave his life to Christ. For the first time in three years since he began working at the bank, he found peace. Amelia noticed the change in his life immediately. He told her about his conversion but wanted to be the first to tell his mother. His mother was delighted. Hudson was amazed to hear that she had been praying for his salvation at the very moment that he was saved.

A Changed Life

Hudson had a fresh desire to read the Bible, and sermons now seemed alive. Hudson and Amelia began to visit the poor sections of Barnsley to pass out tracts, inviting people to church. His father had read an article to the family about the vast population of China and the lack of gospel knowledge. His family began to pray that God would send more missionaries and Bibles to China. Hudson

felt an increasing desire to carry the gospel to the Chinese people. He started to read books about China and study the Chinese language. He realized he needed more training, so he spent more hours studying Latin, Greek, and basic Hebrew.

Hudson also began to strengthen his body for the hardships of missionary life by developing a strenuous exercise plan. He began sleeping on the floor instead of a soft bed, as he was unlikely to find soft beds in China. One of the books he read advised future missionaries to China to prepare by getting medical training. This would give him a practical skill that the Chinese people desperately needed. His aunt's brother-in-law, Dr. Hardey, had a medical practice in Hull. He needed an assistant. He was willing to supply Hudson with room, board, a small salary, and access to classes he taught at a local medical school in exchange for being his assistant. Hudson jumped at the opportunity!

Missionary in Training

Dr. Hardey was a dedicated Christian man who recognized potential in Hudson Taylor. He gave him many opportunities to learn. Hudson had learned how to **compound** medicines and dispense them while working with his father. After work, Hudson spent hours studying for the classes Dr. Hardey taught at Hull Medical School. Hudson experienced quite a few chances to learn to trust God for his financial obligations. He began to pray when in need and looked expectantly to see how God would choose to supply.

Feeling the need for more medical training, Hudson moved to London in September 1852. He stayed with his cousin while he attended a surgery course

compound: combine or mix

at London Hospital in Whitechapel. He wanted to live as **frugally** as possible, so he would buy a loaf of brown bread each day and eat half for supper and half for breakfast the next morning. To save more money, he walked back and forth for four miles each day to the hospital. He walked to church every Sunday.

frugally: inexpensively

malignant fever: probably yellow fever

One day, after observing students who were dissecting the body of a man who had died of **malignant fever**, he began to feel weak and very sick. He had pricked himself with a pin the previous night. The infection had entered his body through that pin prick. The surgeon examined him, then quietly told him that he was going to die and that he should get home as soon as possible. He told the surgeon, "I'm not afraid to die. In fact, I look forward to meeting my Maker. But unless I'm much mistaken, I cannot die because God had called me to China, and I have not been there yet. I may get very sick, but I doubt that I will die."[39]

Hudson did go back to his cousin's home. He was too weak to walk, so he rode on a horse-drawn cart. His uncle Benjamin sent for one of the best doctors in London. He told Hudson it would be a long battle before he recovered, but it might be possible. His uncle Benjamin and cousin Tom took turns caring for him. It was many days before he began to slowly regain enough strength to sit up in bed. He was finally well enough to travel to his parents' home to fully recover. He did not have the funds to make the trip, so he resorted again to prayer, and miraculously, God provided. His doctor commented, "I would give all the world to have a faith like yours."[40] Hudson made a full recovery with the good care he received from his family. It was good to be home again.

Sailing to China

In 1853, the Chinese Evangelization Society contacted Hudson. Conditions in China seemed to be more open-minded to white people entering the country. The society decided the time was right to send two missionaries there immediately. So, on September 19, 1853, Hudson boarded the *Dumfries*, a ship hired to sail from Liverpool, England, to Shanghai, China. Hudson, age 21, waved furiously to his teary-eyed family standing on the dock. At last, Hudson was on his way to China.

becalmed: at a standstill for lack of wind

By Christmastime, the ship had sailed 14,500 miles but still had quite a way to go. They almost met with disaster when the ship became **becalmed**. The captain and crew had given up hope. Hudson had an idea. "Four of us on board are now Christians. Let us each retire to his own cabin and pray to the Lord to give us, immediately, a breeze. He can send one, I know He can!"[41] After just a few minutes, Hudson felt assured the prayer would be answered. He came on deck and told the sailors to let the mainsail down to prepare for the wind that was about to come. The first officer **scoffed**, but as he did so, a strong gust of wind blew, and all hands were called on deck. The ship was on its way again to Shanghai.

scoffed: ridiculed scornfully

British Consulate: offices of British government in foreign nations

shillings: British money

Arriving in China

On Wednesday, March 1, 1854, after five long months at sea, Hudson stepped out of the boat onto Chinese soil. Hudson found his way to the **British Consulate** to check his mail. He expected to find a check and instructions from the Chinese Evangelistic Society. There was no mail waiting for him. He had only a few **shillings** in his pocket and was unsure about what to do next. He located the local missionary hospital and was invited to stay there until he received his instructions. He learned that a bloody civil war had begun, and hundreds of homes had been destroyed. Foreigners were sometimes suspected of being spies. This was not at all what he had expected to find.

Mandarin: official language of China

tutelage: instruction

Thankfully, Hudson met up with Dr. Medhurst, a missionary with the London Missionary Society. He strongly suggested that Hudson learn the **Mandarin** dialect of the Chinese language, which was widely understood throughout the country. Dr. Medhurst arranged for a tutor for Hudson. Hudson learned very quickly. Dr. Medhurst saw much potential in Hudson. Since Hudson was still waiting for instructions from the Chinese Evangelization Society, Dr. Medhurst invited him to continue his medical studies at the London Missionary Hospital under his **tutelage**. So, Hudson spent his days caring for patients and his evenings studying the language.

Inland China

During the next year, Hudson had several opportunities to travel to inland China. "He understood that to truly connect with the people, he needed to embrace their way of life, their traditions, and their language."[42] He had the front part of his head shaved, dyed the rest of his hair black, and obtained Chinese clothing. He was now a blue-eyed Chinaman! He no longer drew a crowd of curious onlookers staring at his strange appearance. He also concluded that if China were to be reached for the gospel, he needed to train Chinese Christians and equip them to spread the gospel to their own people. He started a church in a house on Bridge Street at Ning-po. Here, he planned to train Chinese Christians.

Hudson met and fell in love with Maria Dyer, whose parents had been missionaries in Singapore. The couple married on January 20, 1858. While Hudson spent his energies establishing the church, Maria opened a small school for girls. The couple was very happy and soon had a baby daughter named Grace.

Dr. Parker, a fellow laborer of Hudson's, was a missionary running the hospital in Ning-po. His wife contracted **cholera** and died suddenly. Dr. Parker decided to leave China with their four children and return to Scotland, where his parents could help raise the family. There were no other qualified doctors in Ning-po, so it looked like the hospital would have to close. Dr. Parker encouraged Hudson to take over. Although he did not have adequate training, he and Maria prayed and decided to take on the responsibility. Dr. Parker left them with enough money to run the hospital for one month. Miraculously, they received a check from a man in England who offered to send more money when needed. Church members volunteered their time to help at the hospital — cleaning and sharing the gospel. Hudson was thrilled to see the Chinese people he had trained reaching out to lead others to the Lord. Bridge Street Church continued to grow, and many came to learn about the gospel. Hudson spent his afternoons teaching the Bible to new believers.

cholera: an acute diarrheal infection

tuberculosis: a lung disease

Tuberculosis

Hudson had not been feeling well for quite a while. He tried to ignore the fact that he was getting weaker, but finally he went to the doctor. He was diagnosed with **tuberculosis**. The doctor said he must leave China and go

dialect: a region's specific language

back to England to try to recover. He and Maria took their five children and sailed home. There was a warm family reunion with his parents, sisters, aunts, and uncles. Hudson still invested his energies in China. He resumed his medical studies as soon as he was able. He also began translating the New Testament into the Ning-po **dialect**. He recruited workers to go to Ning-po to help run the Bridge Street Chapel, as the church was now called. It took him four years to complete the translation and receive his medical degree. Dr. Parker remarried and returned to China to run the hospital. During these four years, Hudson and Maria had no steady income. They relied completely on prayer and God's provision for their family.

Missionaries for China

Hudson was intensely aware that more missionaries had to be sent to China. Every month, over one million Chinese people were dying without the Lord Jesus. On June 25, 1865, he wrote in the back of his Bible, "Prayed for twenty-four willing, skillful laborers."[43] The following day he went to the bank and with only ten pounds, opened an account by the name of China Inland Mission. He explained later, "It was 10 pounds and all the promises of God."[44] He wrote a booklet called *China's Spiritual Need and Claims*. In the booklet, he explained how four hundred million Chinese people had never heard the gospel and how it was the duty of other Christians to go into all the world and share the gospel. The booklet became a bestseller and was reprinted many times. Workers and money began to flood in from many sources. On May 26, 1866, Hudson, Maria, their family, and 16 missionaries set sail for China. The China Inland Mission began its work.

They decided to settle in Hang-Chow this time. The city was home to one million people. Hudson located a house at Number One New Lane, a massive building in need of much repair. It had more than 30 rooms. Hudson could foresee a hospital and **dispensary** downstairs with the living area upstairs. The outside was perfect for children, complete with a rock garden and pond and plenty of room to play. The missionaries set to work repairing the damage. The Chinese people were curious and would come to watch them work. Soon they were making new friends.

dispensary: a place medicines are prepared

When the hospital opened, it was not long before they were providing medical care to more than 200 people every day. Hudson had the habit of taking a break by bursting out in song after an especially difficult surgery, such as removing cataracts. Then he would climb upon a desk and preach away. This amused the Chinese people. Maria calmed anxious patients and read Bible stories to the children. Four other mission stations were started in nearby cities. The China Inland Mission continued to grow, and more mission stations were started. Hudson and Maria traveled to encourage all the new mission stations.

Sadly, Maria died after giving birth to their ninth child. Hudson took comfort in the fact that they would spend eternity together in heaven. He continued to build China Inland Mission and recruit missionaries. He traveled to New Zealand, Australia, and even the United States. At Carnegie Hall in New York, he spoke to 3,500 people, including President Woodrow Wilson.

When Hudson was 72 years old, he and his son Howard, now a medical doctor, traveled together to Hudson's beloved China. It was his 11th journey. Chinese Christians made him a large red banner that said, "O man greatly beloved!"[45]

Fifty-four years after he had first come to China, there were over 18,000 Chinese Christians; China Inland Mission had 825 missionaries. On June 3, 1905, Hudson Taylor died quietly in his bed. He was buried beside his wife Maria's grave in China, where his heart belonged. As he once wrote to his sister Amelia, "If I had a thousand pounds, China should have it. If I had a thousand lives, China should have them. No! Not China, but Christ. Can we do too much for Him?"[46]

5

Amy Carmichael

Rescuing Children for Jesus

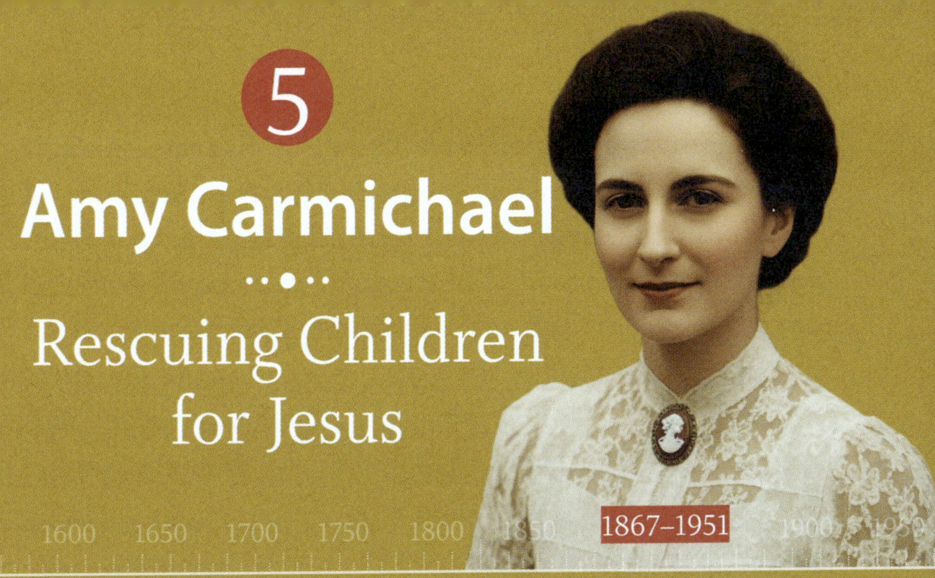

"When my days' work is done on earth, take me straight Home."[47]

Millisle, Ireland – She was born into a family that read the Bible daily. After the family moved to Belfast, Amy's father died, leaving them with financial uncertainty.

Belfast, Ireland – Amy began actively seeking to do God's work; she created two children's ministries and sought to help women living in the slums.

Bangalore, India – Sickness delayed her chance at missions work, but she eventually went to India. She began rescuing child slaves from Hindu temples.

Dohnavur, India – Schools were formed, Amy wrote numerous books, and founded a hospital. She was a bedridden "prayer warrior" for 20 years, dying in 1952.

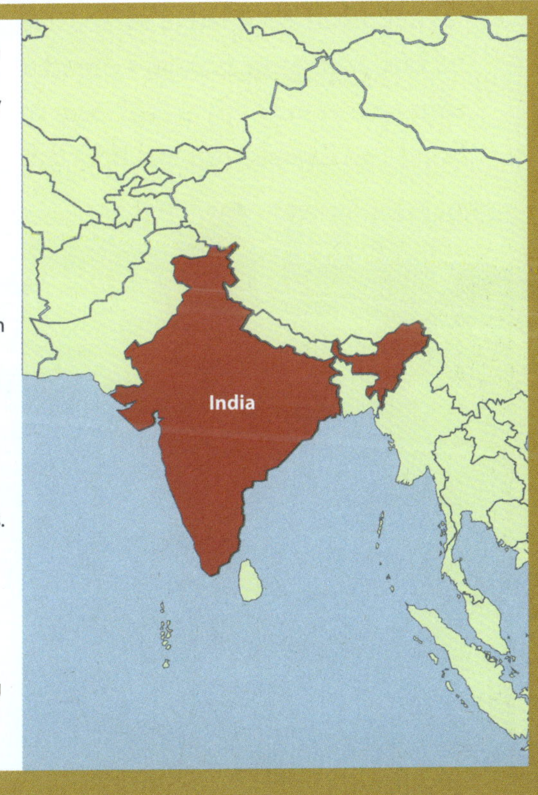

Who Was Amy Carmichael?

Amy Carmichael was an Irish Christian who became a missionary in India. She served in India for 55 years. During this time, she opened an orphanage and rescued children, becoming like a mother to them. She wrote 35 books during her lifetime about her work as a missionary.

Early Years

Amy Carmichael was born on December 16, 1867, in Millisle, Ireland. She was the oldest child of David and Catherine Carmichael and had two younger sisters and four brothers. Her parents were owners of a very successful flour mill. They taught their children from the Bible daily and brought them faithfully to church each Sunday. Amy was born with an adventurous spirit. She was always ready for a challenge. One thing always bothered her as a child, though. She wished for blue eyes; hers were brown. Her mother comforted her by telling her God never makes mistakes

when He creates each person. It was not until years later that Amy realized God had given her brown eyes so He could use her to accomplish a **unique** mission.

unique: unusual, special

pondered: thought about

Moving to Belfast

When Amy was 15, her parents' milling business slowed down. That led them to move the family to the booming city of Belfast. Amy loved exploring the city. She attended a private school to study painting, singing, and music.

Amy's father became sick and died when she was 17. Suddenly, life changed drastically. The family could no longer afford servants. Amy, being the oldest, had to help her mother tutor the younger children, and clean and manage the house. One Sunday on the way home from church, Amy and her siblings noticed a poor beggar woman struggling to haul a bag of sticks. They all helped her carry them home. At first, Amy felt a bit embarrassed to be seen all dressed in her Sunday best helping the raggedly-dressed woman. A Bible passage popped into her head, "Now if any man build upon this foundation gold, silver, precious stones, wood, hay, stubble; Every man's work shall be made manifest: for the day shall declare it, because it shall be revealed by fire; and the fire shall try every man's work of what sort it is" (1 Corinthians 3:12–13). As Amy **pondered** the meaning of the verse for her life, she concluded that from now on she would not waste time with things unimportant in God's eyes. She would live to please Him.

Amy had always been kind to animals and people, but there was a noticeable change in her life now. Her sisters called it "Amy's

enthusiasms."[48] Amy was enthusiastic that there were so many people God wanted her to love, to demonstrate kindness, and with whom to share the good news of the gospel.

New Ministry

Amy Carmichael began holding a children's meeting every Sunday afternoon. She invited the local children to come. She would lead them in singing, tell them Bible stories, and assure them of God's love. Her mother supported her efforts by serving the children lemonade and sandwiches. Many children showed an interest in God's Word. Amy then began holding Saturday morning meetings, which she titled "Morning Watch Club." She encouraged the children to commit to reading the Bible daily and spending time in prayer.

Along with her friend Eleanor Montgomery, she started a night school for boys who worked in factories during the day. She taught them how to read and write and, of course, shared God's Word and prayed with them. Eleanor's father, Dr. Montgomery, admired her enthusiasm and invited her to accompany him on Saturday evenings when he visited the **slums**.

slums: dirty, overcrowded streets inhabited by poor people

Amy was thrilled to go with him and saw many things she'd never seen before. Beggars on the streets, horrible smells, and desperate people were everywhere. Amy and Dr. Montgomery walked the streets handing out bread and gospel tracts. Amy was shocked to see young women about her own age and some much younger, with shawls wrapped around their heads, begging for food. Dr. Montgomery explained that these women often worked 14 hours a day in Irish linen mills. They were paid very poorly and frequently had to beg for food after work each day. Because they didn't have enough money to buy hats, they pulled the shawls around their heads for warmth; thus, they were given the name "shawlies." Amy became convinced that she must begin Sunday morning meetings for the shawlies. She obtained permission from her pastor to hold meetings in the church for them. After two years, the group had grown to more than 400 women.

The Tin Tabernacle

Amy began to look for a larger building in which to hold her meetings. She saw an advertisement for a large building made of iron. It would take

pounds: standard unit of money used in England

500 **pounds** to buy and assemble it. She told her shawlies, and they all committed to praying for the money to purchase the building and for land on which to locate it. While visiting upper-class ladies from the church with her mother, she met Kate Mitchell. Kate expressed much interest in what Amy was doing. She offered to pay for the entire cost of the building! In her search for land, Amy approached the owner of a large lot, told him what she needed it for, and asked his price. To her amazement, he told her an amount that was only one-tenth of its value. God had provided again. Soon there was an iron building on Cambria Street that could seat 500 people. It was called "The Welcome," but most people called it the "Tin Tabernacle." The daily schedule filled up as Amy offered Bible classes, sewing lessons, singing practice, night school, mothers' meetings, girls' meetings, prayer meetings, and of course, gospel meetings.

Moving to England

Although "The Welcome" was prospering, the Carmichaels' finances were not. An old friend offered Mrs. Carmichael a job running a women's rescue shelter near Manchester, England. He also volunteered to support Amy if she agreed to start a ministry among mill workers there. Amy hated to leave "The Welcome," but Kate Mitchell offered to become director of the center, and she knew the ministry there would flourish under Kate's direction.

So, Amy and her mother set sail for England. Amy did not know it then, but that was the last time she would see her homeland of Ireland. Amy decided to rent a room in the slums to live among the shawlies of England. Her ministry grew and things went well for about a year. Then Amy became very sick. A family friend, Robert Wilson, was a wealthy coal miner who invited her to stay with him at Broughton Grange. Here she would benefit from his cook's good food and healthy country air.

Amy soon got stronger and began to help her host with letter writing, entertaining, and organizing. Robert Wilson started to treat Amy like a daughter. At Wilson's home, she also met Hudson Taylor and George Mueller. She was inspired by their testimonies. Amy organized Bible studies for local girls; she also visited surrounding villages and held gospel meetings, and she helped her mother at the rescue mission. Things were going very well, but Amy felt that God wanted her to go to a foreign field. She applied to go to China but was turned down. She had to have a physical examination, and the doctor said her body was still in a weakened state from the illness she had acquired while living in the slums of England. He told her that in China, she would be exposed to typhoid and yellow fever, which flourished there. Any one of them would be too much for her body to handle. The door to China was closed. She then spent 17 months in Japan as a missionary, but her old illness flared up again, and she was forced to return to England to recover.

Amy Goes to India

Amy received a letter from a friend who was a nurse at a mission run by the Zenana Mission Society in India. She asked Amy to consider coming to Bangalore in Southern India where the weather was mild, having none of the extremes of China or Japan. Amy decided to apply and was accepted. Three months later, she was aboard the ship headed for Madras on the coast of India. Robert Wilson, her dear friend, had arranged for his friend Mr. Arden to

dengue fever: a mosquito-born viral infection with flu-like symptoms and fever ranging from mild to severe

Tamil: an official language of India

meet her and help her get settled. Mr. Arden was there when Amy arrived. He loaded her luggage and drove her to his home. She would stay there for three weeks to rest before heading to Bangalore. It was a 230-mile train trip from Madras to Bangalore.

During the trip, Amy came down with **dengue fever**. When she finally arrived, she could hardly get out of her seat. The Zenana missionary who was waiting for her took her straight to the hospital, where she stayed for several weeks.

When Amy was better, she attended a meeting led by Thomas Walker, the chairman of the Church Missionary Society in India. It required traveling to a retreat 3,000 feet up in the Nilgiri Hills. She was fascinated by his words. After the meeting, Mr. Walker invited Amy to live with him and his wife so they could teach her the **Tamil**. Amy started wearing a sari, the traditional dress of Indian women. This was a way to embrace their culture and connect with the women she was trying to reach with the gospel. Eventually, Amy gathered a small group of Indian women willing to step out of their cultural roles to help spread the gospel. The women chose the name "Starry Cluster" for themselves.

Starry Cluster

Daniel 12:3 says, "And they that be wise shall shine as the brightness of the firmament; and they that turn many to righteousness as the stars forever and ever." The women prayed that they would be used to turn Hindu people to righteousness. Around

bandy: a springless cart pulled by two bulls

Christmas 1897, they began traveling on a **bandy**. It was an exhausting way to travel and because it had no springs, the passengers felt every bump in the road.

Most of the villages were surrounded by walls. The women would set up camp just outside the walls. Early in the morning they would enter the marketplace, divide into pairs, and sit under a tree and pray while they waited. Frequently a woman or group of women would saunter over and ask them questions. At lunchtime, they would head back to camp, eat, do a Bible study, and pray for the women they had talked to in the morning. After lunch, they headed back to the marketplace. Usually, they would sing, accompanied by a small organ they carried with them. Then they would teach the gospel in the open air. Amy was training her group of women to be real missionaries. It was customary to give Christian workers a daily allowance called a "batta." When Amy tried to pay the women, they asked her to keep the money for the mission work.

Rescuing the Girls

Amy was about to start a brand-new ministry she could never have dreamed of. The priests of the Hindu temples had a terrible practice of keeping girls as slaves for use in the worship of their false gods. Some widows who felt they could not afford to raise their daughters would even bring their

daughters as babies to the temple to be doomed to live as slaves.

ethnicity: common cultural traditions and ancestry

One day unexpectedly, a girl named Preena escaped from the temple and found her way to Amy. She told her sad story, and Amy refused to return her to the temple. Preena stayed with Amy. Soon Amy was called the "child-stealing Ammai." Ammai was the word for "well-loved mother." Amy became like a mother to Preena. She came to believe that God was calling her to rescue other girls who were experiencing mistreatment at the hands of the idol-worshiping temple workers.

As part of her plan to save the enslaved girls, Amy decided to go to the temples in disguise. She dyed her skin to look like she was of Indian **ethnicity**. She clearly remembered as a three-year-old girl praying for blue eyes. She had been so disappointed to wake up the next morning to see her eyes were still brown. Now, she understood why God had given her brown eyes, even though her siblings' eyes were blue. The all-knowing God had a special plan for Amy's life. If she had blue eyes, she would not have been able to rescue more than 1,000 little girls. As Amy explained, "When I've been out searching for temple children, blue eyes would have been a giveaway that I was a foreigner."[49]

Not only did Amy rescue them, but she became like a mother to the girls. The Tamil language had a saying, "Children tie the mother's feet."[50] It meant that when a woman becomes a mother, she is no longer free to come and go as she used to do. She must stay home with her children. Amy realized that God had tied her feet to care for her "children." Mothering was the main ministry for this season of her life.

Amy taught the girls how to read, write, and spell. She also taught them skills they would need to know as adults. The older girls learned to help with the younger girls. She hired people to grow vegetables and to cook and clean. She followed the example set by George Mueller. Whenever a need arose, Amy began to pray, and money and supplies would start coming in.

They settled in the village of Dohnavur, where God provided an entire school compound previously used by a former missionary.

It was a safe place to raise children. Amy sent letters all over India to pastors and missionaries to let them know they could bring any rescued temple children to Amy, who was eager to take them in. By June 1904, Amy had 17 girls. In response to her letters, she soon had to build a nursery to accommodate babies that were rescued and brought to her.

drudgery: hard, unpleasant work

Boys Are Added to the Family

Eventually, Amy began taking in baby boys, saving them from a life of temple **drudgery**. Eight years later, in 1926, there were 80 boys, from newborn to 14. That year, God sent her more male missionaries to help care for the boys. Amy was now 60 years old. She began to pray for money to build a hospital to care for sick children. The hospital would also provide jobs for young men and women in Amy's "family." The cost for a hospital was ten thousand pounds. Amy began to pray for funds. On June 28, 1928, one thousand pounds arrived in the mail. The rest of the money came in smaller amounts. The children even helped to raise funds. When the hospital was finally finished, people came from miles around for treatment, and the Dohnavur "family" ministered to them all. Many of Amy's "children" became Christians and grew up to serve in the orphanage or hospital that had rescued them.

Tragedy Strikes

A house located in nearby Kalakadu had been empty for many years. It was offered to Amy. She and one of her nurses planned to turn it into a dispensary. While Amy was inspecting the progress at the construction site, dusk set in. She stepped out of the house and fell into a large hole dug by a construction worker. She felt a stabbing pain shoot up her leg and found she could not put weight on it. She was taken 46 miles to the main hospital. Amy, now 63 years old, had broken her leg. Arriving back in Dohnavur, she found walking very painful. Her leg was healing, but she had also hurt her back in the fall. Amy developed arthritis and became crippled. For the next 20 years, she could not walk more than a few steps or be out of bed for more than an hour at a time.

Being disabled was difficult for Amy to accept. It was she who had given her life to serving others. Twenty years before she had written in her journal, "Lord, teach me how to conquer pain. When my days' work is done on earth, take me straight Home. Do not let me be ill and a burden or anxiety to anyone. Let me not die of a lingering illness. Father, forgive me if this prayer is wrong."[51]

Amy's Last Days

As time passed, Amy learned the answer to that prayer had been "No." However, just as God had a reason for Amy to have brown eyes, he had a reason for her disability now. The children learned valuable lessons as they observed how she dealt with her problems. She always said, "It is the trial of our faith."[52] Amy's friends made her bedroom into a **sanctuary**. She called it her "Room of Peace." They brought in many books for her to read and a giant birdcage filled with finches and canaries. Outside her window, they planted colorful flowering plants in a beautiful garden.

sanctuary: place of rest

Amy made remarkable use of her time in bed. She began writing and authored 35 books about her time as a missionary. Her books were translated into many languages and distributed all over the world. Her writing inspired others to become missionaries, and many came to carry on the work both in Dohnavur and all over the world. She wrote poems and songs and sent many letters.

Amy was a **prayer warrior**. She continued to tell visitors about the glorious gospel of Jesus Christ. From her bed, she gave direction for the ministry and encouragement to all. She was a mother to hundreds of girls and boys and a friend to many. Amy grew weaker and slept longer until on January 18, 1951, a few weeks after her 83rd birthday, she simply did not wake up. She was buried with those of her precious Dohnavur family who had died previously. Her "family" placed a birdbath over her grave bearing one word: "Ammai." The homes and mission work Amy began are still operating today and are run by Indian people. She instructed her workers as she had lived her life, "Forget yourself in serving others. That is the way of joy."[53]

prayer warrior: especially skilled in prayer

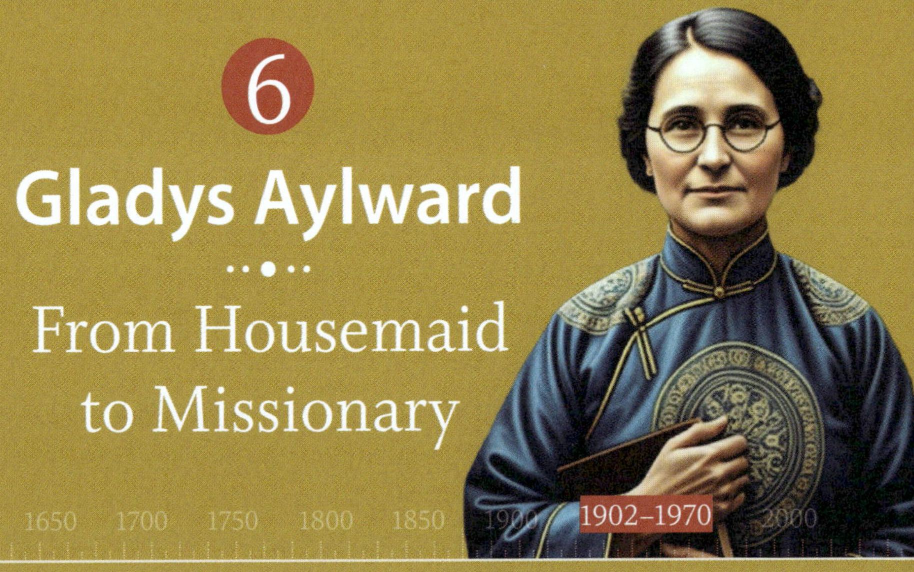

6

Gladys Aylward

From Housemaid to Missionary

> *"I want to go to China to serve you. God, don't let me die here."*[54]

Edmonton, North London – Gladys enjoyed listening to Bible stories and adventures about other places. She left school to be a maid at 14.

London, England – At 25, she felt a call to mission work in China, but she struggled to learn Chinese. Journeying to China in 1930, she ended up in a Russia war zone.

Yangcheng, China – Gladys met Mrs. Lawson; the house became an inn where Gladys learned the language and shared Bible stories with guests.

Fufeng, China – She stopped a prison riot, took care of orphan children, and saved others during a war. Gladys died at 67 in 1970, hours after rescuing a baby.

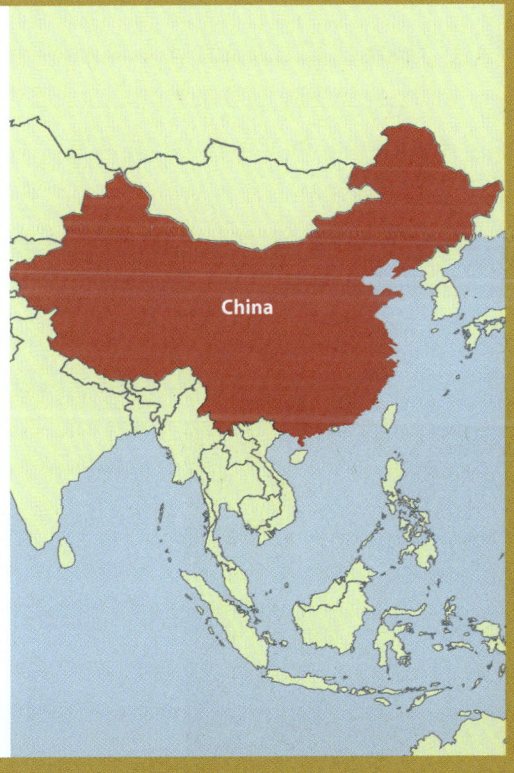

Who Was Gladys Aylward?

Gladys Aylward was working as a housemaid in London when she felt God call her to become a missionary to China. She was accepted by China Inland Missions but failed her Bible class, so for academic reasons, she could not continue her studies there. Convinced that God wanted her to serve in China, she kept working as a housemaid until she saved enough money to pay her own fare. Gladys constantly faced almost impossible circumstances, but she persevered and poured her heart into serving the Chinese. She risked her life many times to help those in need and won the respect of the people of China. Thousands of Chinese were led to the Lord because of her investment of love.

salary: pay for work done

Early Years

Gladys Aylward was born on February 24, 1902, in Edmonton, North London. She was the youngest of three children. Her parents were dedicated Christians who taught their children to love and serve God. Her father was a postman but did not collect an adequate **salary** to support his family. Her mother also worked at the post office sorting mail. Gladys was a happy, energetic child, always ready for a new adventure. She loved listening while her mom told Bible stories each night. Gladys went to Silver Street School but never excelled in her studies. She preferred to read about adventures in exciting places.

For financial reasons, Gladys had to leave school when she was 14 years old to take a position as a housemaid. Her job was cleaning, cooking, and serving wealthy people who lived in huge London mansions. When she was 25 years old, she attended a new church. Here, she listened as a young preacher spoke of China's need for missionaries. That night she strongly felt that God was calling her to be a missionary to China.

When she was 27 years old, she was accepted at the training school of the China Inland Mission Society. After three months, however, the director gently explained to her that her grades were not good enough for her to continue the training. He felt she would never be able to learn the Chinese language. Gladys was devastated but felt sure God had called her to China. The director suggested she work as a housemaid for an elderly missionary couple who had just retired from their ministry in China. At first, Gladys was downcast, but once she met the Fishers, she was excited to learn all they had to share about China. Her desire to devote her life to being a missionary grew. She decided she would have to save enough money to get her own ticket to China.

affluent: wealthy

Saving for China

Since she needed to earn more money, Gladys took a job with an **affluent** family who lived near Buckingham Palace. Upon arrival, she was shown to her very pleasant room and began to unpack her only suitcase. After paying for her train fare from Edmonton to London, she was left with only two and a half pennies. She thought, *If God really does want me to go to China, surely He will help me get the funds.* She placed her money next to her Bible. She prayed, "Here is my Bible. Here is all the money I have. Here is me. Find some way to use me, God."[55] A few minutes later, the lady for whom

reimbursed: paid back

she worked **reimbursed** her for her train fare. She put the three shillings next to the pennies and thanked God.

Gladys had no idea what a ticket to China would cost. She went to Muller's Shipping Agency to find out, intending to put a deposit on her ticket and then keep paying more every week until it was paid. The clerk at the shipping office told her it would cost her 90 pounds. That was outrageous! It would take her much too long to save 90 pounds! She asked if there was a cheaper way. He told her there was — a train route that led through Europe, Russia, Siberia, and finally to Tientsin in Northern China. The cost to travel by rail was just 47 pounds, ten shillings. The only problem was that Russia and China were at war. The clerk told Gladys she might not arrive safely at her destination. Nevertheless, Gladys was determined. She put three pounds down toward the cheaper ticket, thinking that by the time she saved enough money, the war would probably be over. She volunteered to work at banquets and extra events that her employer sponsored to earn money more quickly.

Preparing for Mission Work

Gladys began studying on her own to learn what a missionary should know. She realized she needed to be able to teach people. She often went to Hyde Park in London, stood on wooden boxes, and taught whoever would listen. She told people about the gospel of Jesus Christ and their need to make Him the Lord of their lives. She also studied books about China.

One night after church, a friend told her of a 73-year-old lady, Mrs. Lawson, who had been a missionary to China. She and her husband had come home to England where he died, and she decided to go back to China by herself. Mrs. Lawson had looked for a younger person to accompany her but had been unsuccessful. Gladys excitedly told the friend of her desire to be a missionary to China. The friend gave Gladys Mrs. Lawson's address and wished her luck. Gladys wrote to Mrs. Lawson that evening. It had been seven months since Gladys had started paying for her ticket. Soon, she would have all the funds she needed. Mrs. Lawson wrote back and agreed to meet Gladys in Tientsin.

Gladys Leaves for China

On October 15, 1930, Gladys said her farewells to her family and friends. Even the clerk from Muller's Shipping Agency came to see her off. Gladys climbed aboard the train and waved goodbye. Seven days later, the train was moving through Russia. More and more soldiers were boarding the train. As the train headed southeast toward China, Gladys drifted off to sleep. She awoke to hear the conductor yelling at her in words she could not understand. He seemed to be telling her to get off the train at this stop. She refused and the train moved through Siberia.

war zone: area of dangerous conflict

trudged: walking though exhausted

machinist: person using tools

plight: bad situation

When the train stopped again, she realized this was the final stop and she was in the middle of a **war zone**. She managed to understand that it might be many days before it headed back, carrying wounded men. She would have to walk all the way back to the station where she had refused to get off to continue her journey. The ground was covered with snow, and the cold was biting. She **trudged** along, carrying her suitcase and praying, "I want to go to China to serve you. God, don't let me die here."[56]

After nearly getting frostbite, she finally arrived at the station. She was taken to a small, dirty room by some Russian soldiers. She tried to tell them she was a missionary, but they took her passport and changed the word missionary to **machinist**. She then realized they were trying to kidnap her and make her work in Russian factories. Gladys was terrified but kept praying to God. They put her on a train headed for Vladivostok where the factories were located. There, she was taken to an old hotel. Surprisingly, a girl knocked at her door. She told Gladys she understood her **plight** and would help her escape. That night the girl took her to the docks and helped her climb aboard a ship headed for Japan. Gladys had her luggage, but the Russians had stolen most of her clothes, money, and belongings. When she arrived in Japan, she was directed to a missionary compound where she was fed a hearty meal. The missionaries bought her a boat ticket to Tientsin, China. So, 21 days after leaving London, Gladys was on the last leg of her journey.

Finding Mrs. Lawson

fraught: stressful

When she arrived, Gladys found that Mrs. Lawson was not in Tientsin but had gone to Tsechow in the Shanxi province, far to the west. Gladys felt like bursting into tears. This whole trip had been so **fraught** with unexpected difficulties! She was told that it would take probably another 25 days, first on a train and then more days on several buses, to get to Tsechow. The missionaries in Tientsin were kind and encouraged Gladys to rest before continuing her trip. They fed her well and told her they knew Mrs. Lawson would be delighted to have her help. They even introduced her to a businessman, Mr. Lu, who was headed in the same direction. He agreed to escort Gladys most of the way to Tsechow. Mr. Lu taught her much about China on the trip.

Along the way, they had to stay overnight at an inn. Gladys found that Chinese inns were nothing like inns in England. They consisted of one large room with a platform set up on bricks. The

platform, called a k'ang, was a hard communal bed. That meant that all the guests at the inn slept side by side on the same platform! It was so strange. Everyone wore the clothes that they had been wearing all day, and it was extremely difficult to sleep with many snoring or squirming about. Breakfast was a bowl of soup with noodles and vegetables. It took 25 more days of riding over bumpy roads to finally get to Tsechow.

Once in Tsechow, Gladys asked for the mission. Mrs. Smith, a kind missionary woman, answered the door and invited Gladys in for hot tea. Mrs. Lawson had been there but had relocated and was now two days away, high up in the remote mountain village of Yangcheng. Gladys could hardly believe what she was hearing. There were no buses that went up that mountain. She would have to travel by mule litter. The mule litter was a basket perched on the back of one of the eight mules in the mule train. Her suitcases rode in a basket on another mule. The muleteer was a man who led the mules along the path. On the trip up the mountain, Gladys was jerked and bumped along on the back of the mules. She had to hold the sides of the basket to help buffer the jolts. At night they entered walled villages to be protected from wolves and robbers. At last they arrived, and Gladys' search was over. She met Mrs. Lawson.

A Different Kind of Ministry

dilapidated: run-down

muleteers: person who drives mules

Mrs. Lawson lived in a big, **dilapidated** house. At first, her manner was very gruff, and Gladys began to wonder if she had made a mistake in coming all this way. Mrs. Lawson was the only Christian in the town, and the Chinese were afraid of the white women. Yang, the cook, began to teach Gladys the language. Gladys made the comment that one day she would ride back and forth with the mule train to share the gospel with people along the way. Mrs. Lawson jumped at the idea. "Yes, it's the perfect answer. We'll turn this house into an inn. We can't get people into a church, but we can get them into an inn, especially if it's the cleanest inn on the whole trail. We get the **muleteers** in, water their mules for them, feed the men a good meal, and then offer them something no other inn does."[57] Mrs. Lawson said she would tell them Bible stories for free. The Chinese people loved stories. She was sure they would retell the stories to everyone on the trail. She was thrilled with the idea. This was a project that excited Gladys!

The women began cleaning the old house and converting it into an inn. They called it "Inn of Eight Happinesses." They chose this name because they wanted to offer eight things that other inns did not have: love, virtue, gentleness, tolerance, truth, loyalty, beauty, and devotion. They hoped this would make the muleteers ask questions and want to hear more about Jesus. Gladys would meet the muleteers when they arrived in town and tell them in Chinese, "We have no fleas, we have no bugs. Come! Come! Good! Good!"[58]

Yang would cook meals, and Mrs. Lawson would tell Bible stories, leaving caring for the mules to Gladys. It was a slow process getting

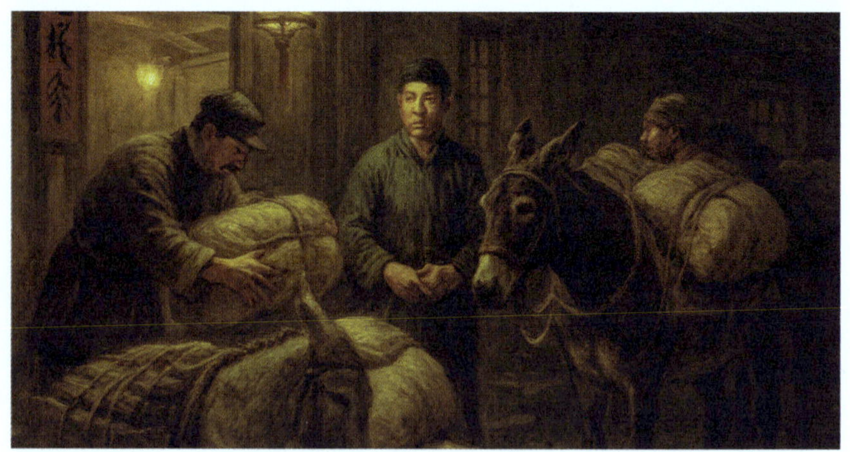

the muleteers to trust the white women, but once one group was brave enough, word spread quickly. Gladys worked hard to learn the language; fortunately, she was able to do so quickly. Soon she was telling Bible stories to the Chinese.

Alone to Carry On

One day, Mrs. Lawson fell off a balcony and was seriously injured. Gladys nursed her wounds, but unfortunately, Mrs. Lawson died soon after. Gladys was left to carry on the ministry by herself.

About a week later, the **Mandarin** came looking for Gladys. He told her he needed her help. A new government in Nanking has passed a ruling that an ancient practice must be stopped. **Footbinding** was a practice the Chinese had enforced for years. They thought small feet on women were beautiful, but it was a painful practice that resulted in lifelong disabilities. The Mandarin wanted her to travel to all the villages, spreading the news that footbinding

Mandarin: a high public official who ruled mountainous villages

footbinding: tightly wrapping the feet of young girls

must be stopped. Gladys was to help the women and girls remove the bindings and teach them how to walk. The Mandarin told her he needed a woman brave enough to travel over rough roads and climb mountains to reach all the villages. Only a woman with unbound feet could manage that task. He told her she was the only woman who could do all that and also speak the language. He sent two of his officers to travel with her for protection, and he gave her a mule to ride. He also offered to pay her for her services.

excellency: a title of high status

Gladys thought it was a perfect opportunity to share the gospel message. "Wherever I went on behalf of your **excellency**, I would speak of my God and my faith, and I would try to make others believe as I do."[59] The Mandarin said that arrangement was okay with him, and he bowed in respect to Gladys. God had provided a way for her to make a living while sharing the gospel! Women and girls were very grateful to her, and many became Christians.

Prison Riot

One evening, a messenger from the Mandarin arrived at her door, asking Gladys to hurry to the prison. The prisoners were rioting and killing each other; the Mandarin wanted Gladys to stop the mayhem. The magistrate explained why he sent for her: "You say you have the living God inside of you. They can't kill you. You must stop them!"[60]

Though fearing for her life, Gladys braced herself and went inside. She shouted at the prisoners to stop and said she would help them. To her amazement, they did stop. She asked why they were fighting and discovered that it was mainly to protest the terrible

treatment they received. They were starving, despairing of life, and frightened. She promised to try to get the Mandarin to agree to improve conditions. The Mandarin implemented the improvements she suggested. The prisoners were now allowed to bathe, wash their clothes, and grind grain for their food. Work was provided to fill their days, which gave them a source of income. News about Gladys and her achievements spread, and the Chinese gave her a new name, "'Ai-weh-deh," which meant "the righteous one." Her reputation grew, and people loved her. As time went on, Gladys began adopting children who had no mothers. She soon had five children to look after. She was asked to start a school for children, and she did so quite successfully.

War Comes

In 1937, Japanese troops began moving into China. In 1938, bombs fell on Yangcheng, destroying buildings and killing many. Gladys was trapped but not hurt. She began rescuing other trapped people as soon as she was helped from the rubble. The children had been in school during the attack and were safe. Gladys organized the townspeople to care for one another. Then, the Mandarin came with the chilling news that Japanese troops would be in their village in two days. Everyone had to **evacuate**. Gladys was now responsible for about 40 people — her children, some new converts, and more children made orphans because of the attack. Her travels as a foot inspector enabled Gladys to know the area well. She led her people to Bei Chai Chung, a hidden location with no roads leading directly to it. It was surrounded by many caves and places to hide. She had made friends with the people there and knew they would be willing to share food.

evacuate: leave the town

It took Gladys and her people a full day of climbing to get there. The Mandarin, knowing he was in danger, joined them on the journey. They were all tired when they arrived, but here they were safe. One day while they were there, the Mandarin invited Gladys and the residents of Bei Chai Chung to a dinner because he had an announcement to make. To Gladys' surprise, he stood and said, "Ai-weh-deh, Ai-weh-deh, my dear friend Ai-weh-deh, I have seen

all that you are and all that you do, and I would like to become a Christian like you."[61] Tears flooded Gladys' eyes. In the middle of all the violence and war, God had been working in the heart of the Mandarin. It was worth all the adversity!

Rescuing 100 Children

The fighting continued for three years. Children kept coming to Ai-weh-deh. Eventually, she had more than 100 children in her care. Then, news came that the Japanese had retreated from Yangcheng. Gladys moved back to the Inn of Eight Happinesses and began repairing the damage. One day, a newspaper reporter from America came to interview her. He had heard of Ai-weh-deh and asked her many questions. She answered, hoping it would make more people aware of the tremendous needs in China. Little did she ever dream that the article would be published on the front page of *Time* magazine and read by millions of people around the world. Unfortunately, it was read by the Japanese also, and now there was a price on Gladys' head.

The Japanese High Command offered a reward for Gladys' capture. At the same time, the children had to be moved to safety. Gladys would not leave without them. She prayed that night for direction. In the morning, she told all the children to put on every piece of clothing they had and grab their bedrolls. Gladys packed up what food was left, and they set off for Sian and safety. Sometimes, Gladys led the children in singing to make the **arduous** trek seem lighter. By the 12th day, they reached Sian. To their **dismay**, they learned that the gates to the city were closed and no more refugees were allowed in. The

arduous: very difficult

dismay: disappointment, fear

children's feet were sore and tired. They were all exhausted, and Gladys was growing very sick.

Gladys was told there was an orphanage in Fufeng that could be reached by train. They trudged on to the train station. Yes, there was a train, but the cars were full of coal. It was not a passenger train. Gladys begged the station master to let the children climb aboard the coal. He gave her permission, and the children scrambled up the mounds of black, dusty coal. Amid all of this, Gladys was growing sicker. She sometimes even forgot where she was and what she was doing. At last, they arrived at Fufeng. The children were safe! They would be cared for here. With God's help, Gladys had done what everyone thought was impossible. She had delivered 100 children from death at the hands of the pursuing Japanese army. With all that accomplished, Gladys collapsed. She was taken to the hospital, suffering from pneumonia, typhoid, exhaustion, and malnutrition. It took her six months to partially recover.

Gladys Presses On

When she felt better, Gladys gathered her adopted children and decided to make a home for them in Fufeng. She and the children prayed for funds. The local Methodist church came to her rescue. They needed people to help with the refugee work and asked Gladys to join them in exchange for their support. She spoke at prisons, leper camps, hospitals, and to students at the local university. More than 200 students became Christians. As news of her success spread, it became dangerous for her to remain there. She left for Shanghai. The doctors at Shanghai recommended that she return to England to fully recover and rest, free from the threat of being captured by the advancing Japanese.

Gladys was delighted to see her family again. It was wonderful. But it was a total shock when she realized she was now famous all over the world. The British Broadcasting Corporation had told her story of escape over the treacherous mountains with 100 children in a war hero series they produced. There was a radio play about her life, as well as a best-selling biography entitled *The Small Woman.* A Hollywood movie of her story was produced. Everyone knew her name. "She even met Queen Elizabeth, an amazing event, she joked, for an English parlour-maid."[62]

Gladys used her fame to spread the word about helping China. She traveled all over England and raised money for Chinese refugees since many were coming to England. She established collection centers to provide them with clothing. By 1949, the Chinese Communists had taken over China. It broke her heart that she, the now famous Gladys Aylward, could not return. She did, however, go to Taiwan, a Chinese island about 100 miles off the coast of China. It had not been taken over by the Communists, and many Chinese people fled there for refuge.

Final Days

In 1957, Gladys said her last farewell to her mother and headed for Taiwan. There, she established orphanages, taught Bible classes, and shared the gospel. She spent the last 14 years of her life in Taiwan, ministering to the Chinese people. On New Year's Day in 1970, someone brought her a newborn baby who had been abandoned by its mother. She gladly accepted the child, bathed it, fed it, and tucked it in the crib beside her bed. That night, Gladys Aylward, age 67, fell asleep to wake up in the arms of Jesus.

7

Eric Liddell

Champion for God

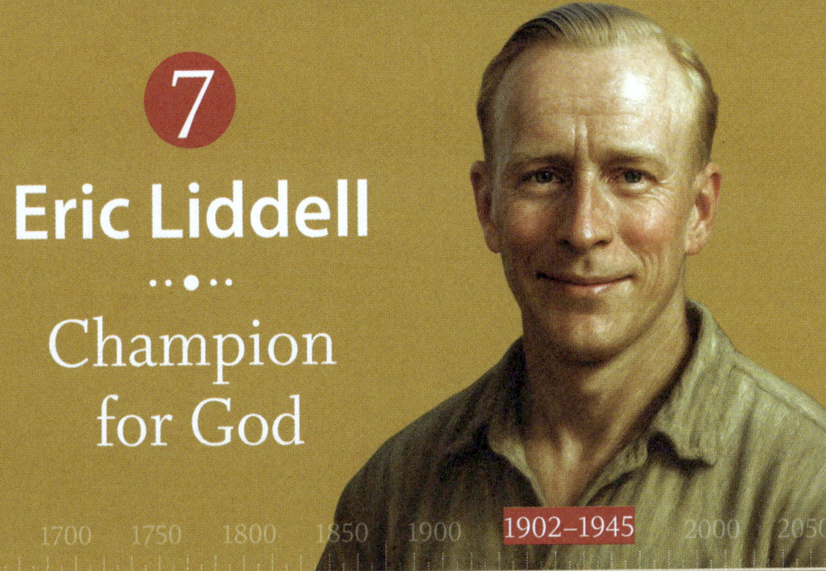

"... each one of us is in a greater race than I have ever run ... and this race ends when God gives out the medals."[63]

Tientsin, China – Though Scottish, Eric was born in China in 1902, where his missionary family was working. His father was a pastor; his mother was a nurse.

London, England – Eric and his brother Robert were left in London to study at a boarding school for children of missionaries.

Edinburgh, Scotland – In 1923, Eric used athletic skill to open doors to share the gospel. He also won a gold medal and gave credit to God. Then he chose to return to China.

Siaochang, China – He cared for the wounded and shared God's truth. Eric died in an internment camp in 1945. He helped sow faith seeds that still grow in China.

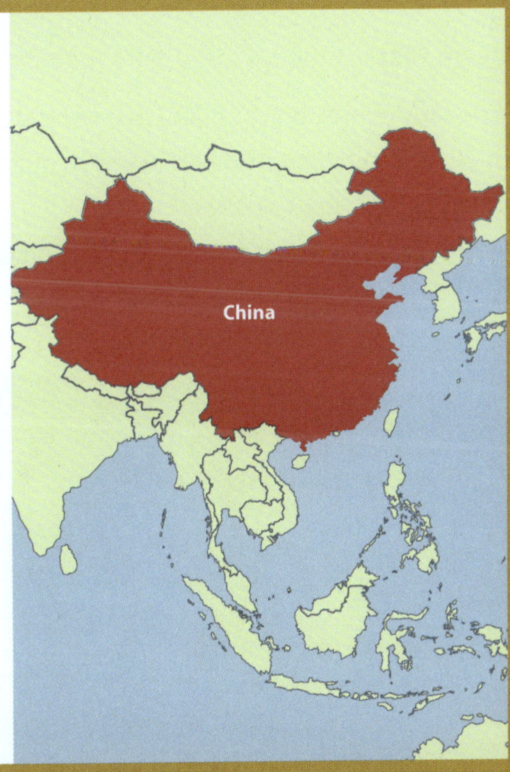

Who Was Eric Liddell?

Eric Liddell was a Scottish athlete who became a Christian missionary. As a young man, he set a world record for the 400-meter race at the Olympics held in 1924. He was the first Scotsman ever to win an Olympic gold medal. As he explained to his fans, God called him to a more significant race — one where God gives out the medals. He committed his life to being a missionary to China. Having been raised in China by missionary parents, he had determined to one day return to share the gospel of his Lord Jesus Christ. Millions of Chinese people had never heard the good news. He poured out his life for them and died as a prisoner of the Japanese during World War II.

Early Years

Eric Liddell was born on January 16, 1902, in the city of Tientsin, in Northern China. His parents were of Scottish descent and had devoted their lives as missionaries to the Chinese people. Shortly after Eric was born, the London Missionary Society relocated his

family to a missionary compound in Sio Chang, China. The Great Plain of China surrounded Sio Chang and was home to ten million people living in ten thousand villages, all crowded together. There were four large houses inside the **compound** walls, along with two schools, one for girls and one for boys. At school, the boys learned both Chinese and English. Eric loved playing with his Chinese friends. Four-year-old Eric, along with his six-year-old brother Robert and younger sister Jenny, enjoyed the free run of the place during the day. At nighttime, the gate to the compound was closed for protection. His father, James, preached in the church, and his mother, Mary, often helped teach in the school. She also was a nurse and tended to many of the local children when they were sick.

compound: buildings in an enclosed area

furlough: a time period of rest

Furlough to England

When Eric was five, the missionary society sent his family home to Scotland for a year's **furlough**. Eric was amazed as the train stopped in Dryman, Scotland. There was so much unoccupied land with lush green pastures for sheep scattered over the countryside. He enjoyed spending time at his grandfather's store and riding with him on his horse-drawn wagon. It was customary for children of missionaries to attend special boarding schools established for them in England. So, at the end of the year, Mr. and Mrs. Liddelll told the two boys they would not be returning to China with their family.

Boarding School

> **disconsolate:** dejected, downcast
>
> **competent:** having adequate abilities

The School for the Sons of Missionaries had about 150 students. Eric was **disconsolate** that his parents and Jenny were leaving for China. He was glad Robert was with him, but the first night at the school, he cried himself to sleep. "Someday I'll go back too. Someday Father and I will work together in China," he promised himself.[64] The school placed a lot of emphasis on sports. Robert and Eric began to excel in athletic competitions. When Eric was 10 years old, he wrote home, "I don't think much of the lessons, but I can run."[65]

By 1918, Robert and Eric were the two star athletes of the school. When one came in first place, the other would come in second place. When Robert graduated, he left for medical school. Eric stayed busy with studies and sports and excelled at both. In his senior year, he passed all his exams and set a record for the 100-yard sprint that has never been broken.

With Rob gone, Eric became more of a leader. He began attending Bible studies regularly. He also started visiting sick folks at a nearby mission. At school, he befriended those boys who were not as **competent** as he was. His early training at home had taught him to hold a high respect for the Christian faith and the importance of setting Sunday apart as a day for the Lord. He did that faithfully.

Edinburgh University

After graduating, Eric went to Edinburgh University. His friend Bill Harvey invited him to participate in the University Athletic Sports competition. Eric entered the 100-yard and 200-yard races.

As a 19-year-old athlete, Eric outran all other students. He was Edinburgh University's best hope of winning a medal at the Scottish University Sports Competition. The more he ran, the more he won, and he seemed to be breaking records every time. People were impressed with not only his speed but also his attitude. Before each race, he always shook his competitors' hands and wished them success.

The year 1923 was a turning point for Eric. He met a young divinity student named D.P. who was seriously involved in evangelism. D.P. challenged Eric to speak to young men at a meeting run by the Glasgow Students' Evangelical Union. Although unsure of his ability to address a group, Eric accepted. He had a relaxed, conversational way of sharing the gospel. Eric later told D.P. that a new joy had come into his life since he first spoke at that meeting. The following week, he was asked to talk to 600 men at a town hall and was well received. He began to see that God could use his fame in athletics as an open door for sharing the gospel of Christ. As he accepted more speaking engagements, it seemed he won more races.

sprinter: athlete who runs short distances

The Olympics

When trials were scheduled for the Olympics in 1924, Eric decided to try out. He was the top **sprinter** in Scotland and broke the British record for the 100-yard dash. This record was unbroken for the next 35 years. He was awarded a place on the British Olympic Team. Newspapers announced he was "Britain's best hope for a gold medal in the 100-meter race."[66]

He also competed in the 440-yard race in Stoke-on-Trent, representing Scotland in a competition against Ireland and England. During this race, J.J. Gillies, a runner from England, was next to Eric. Attempting to get a head start, Gillies bumped into Eric and knocked him down. Eric assumed he was disqualified, but the officials were waving him on. He was now at least 20 feet behind all the other runners. It appeared impossible for him to catch up, but somehow, he managed to run faster and faster. The crowd stood to its feet, cheering him on. With 40 yards to go, he was in fourth place. "Then with a superhuman burst of speed, he dashed across the finish line in the first place."[67] He collapsed and was carried off the field on a stretcher as the crowd rose, cheering their new champion. That day Eric's race was called the greatest quarter-mile performance of all time. He returned to Scotland with a hero's welcome. The Scottish people eagerly awaited the Olympics, wanting to witness their hero win the gold medal in the 100-yard sprint.

An Unexpected Turn of Events

traitor: one who betrays his country

When the schedule came out, however, Eric saw that the 100-yard sprint competition was to take place on a Sunday. Eric would not run on a Sunday. He had been taught as a young boy that Sunday was a day of rest and reverence for God. He would not run, even for the promise of a gold medal! Suddenly, the fans who loved him turned against him. Some called him a **traitor** to his country. He appealed to get the day changed but was turned down. The British Olympic Committee tried to get him to change his mind but, failing, asked him to consider running the 200- and 400-meter races later in the week. He agreed. Many other athletes told him they respected his stand for not running on Sunday.

Temperatures rose in the 100s on the day Eric was to compete in the 400-meter race at the 1924 Olympic games. An old friend encouraged him by handing him a slip of paper. It said, "In the old book it says, 'Them that honour me, I will honour.' Wishing you the best of success, always. I Samuel 2:30."[68] This was not the race Eric usually ran. He knew if he were to win, it would only be with God's help.

Eric started out strong and ended strong. He was the first man to cross the finish line at an amazing world-record pace of 47.6 seconds — the first Scotsman ever to win the gold medal! Eric collapsed into the arms of the British coach, totally exhausted. But

in a few minutes, he stood as the gold medal was draped around his neck. As the band played "God Save the King," his friend Tom came up and congratulated him, saying, "You couldn't just win, you had to go and set a world record!"[69] When interviewed by the press, Eric gave credit to the Lord. "The secret of my success over the 400 meters is that I run the first 200 meters as hard as I can. Then, for the second 200 meters, with God's help, I run harder."[70]

A More Important Race Awaits

A week later, Eric arrived in Edinburgh. He attended a dinner given in his honor. He was now Scotland's most **eminent** sports star. He stood to make a speech and shocked his audience by saying, "It has been a wonderful experience to compete in the Olympic games and to bring home a gold medal. But since I've been a young lad, I have had my eyes on a different prize. You see, each one of us is in a greater race than I have ever run in Paris, and this race ends when God gives out the medals. It has always been my intention to be a missionary, and I have just received word that

eminent: most respected and admired

I have been accepted as a chemistry teacher at the Anglo-Chinese College at Tientsin, China. From now on, I will be putting my energy into preparing to take up that position."[71] The crowd was stunned and silent. Scotland's finest athlete was giving up running to go to China!

Eric decided to stay one more year in Scotland to study theology at the Congregational College in Edinburgh. After all, his ultimate goal in going to China was to share the gospel, and he wanted to be well equipped. He would also teach religion and sports. During that year, he studied diligently but also accepted many speaking engagements. Huge crowds turned out to listen to him.

Before leaving for China, he ran in one more event — the Scottish AAA Championships at Hampton Park, Glasgow. Twelve thousand spectators turned out to watch him run in the 100-, 220-, and 440-yard races. As they cheered him on, Eric astonished the crowds by winning all three races. When he spoke in churches, the crowds turned out; often, 1,000 people had to be turned away for lack of space.

shafts: long pieces of wood that normally hitch to a horse

Off to China

On July 13, 1925, Eric was shocked when his friends and students arrived to drive him to the station in an elaborate carriage. Instead of being pulled by horses, this carriage was led by two teams of students and friends holding the **shafts** and conveying him to the nearby train station. Crowds lined the street to wish him well. Eric spoke a few words: "Our motto should be Christ for the world, for the world needs Christ."[72] Eric boarded the train, leaned out the window, and led the crowd in singing a hymn. A national hero, Eric was giving up his fame and heading to a country where he would be a stranger amid a land **fraught** with revolution and turmoil.

fraught: uneasy

Eric was delighted to meet up again with his family. He lived in his parents' house while he taught at school. The school, for Chinese boys ages 12 to 18, was distinctly Christian. The teaching was done in English. It was the top educational institute in Northern China. Eric helped design a running track for the students — the best track in Asia at the time. He occasionally ran races himself. He also re-learned the Mandarin language he had spoken as a boy.

Marriage and Family

In 1929, Eric's parents retired after working faithfully for 30 years as missionaries. That summer, Eric met Florence MacKenzie. She, too, was a child of missionaries to China. Florence was just 17 years old and committed to becoming a nurse. She planned to go to nursing school in Canada. Before she left, the couple became engaged, realizing it would be four years before they could marry.

During a furlough, Eric went home and was ordained by the Scottish Congregational Church. He did quite a bit of speaking, and of course, visited Florence in Canada before returning to China. In March 1934, Eric and Florence were married. In July 1935, a baby girl was born. In January 1937, their second daughter was born.

Eric Ministers in Siaochang

China's Great Plain was dangerous because of the approaching Japanese armies. Many missionaries were leaving China. The London Missionary Society suggested that Eric be sent to Siaochang, where he had lived for the first five years of his life. However, it was unsafe, and he would have to leave Florence and his two daughters in Tientsin. He wrestled with the decision to go, but Florence reminded him, "Eric, you knew it was wrong to run on Sunday, and you know it's wrong not to go where God has called you. You have no choice but to go."[73]

On his arrival, the Chinese people thanked Eric for coming. They remembered the extraordinary work his parents had done for so many years. Robert, his older brother, was a doctor in the local hospital. Eric's job was to travel to different villages by bicycle, encouraging and helping the people and conducting church services. In 1938, Robert was due to leave on furlough, so Eric learned first aid and began helping at the rescue stations where they treated the wounded before transporting them to the hospital. He insisted on helping all wounded, whether they were Chinese or

occupation: enemy military's seizure of the land

internment camps: camps for civilians during war, especially those with ties to an enemy

Japanese. In February 1940, the mission had to close because of Japanese occupation. Eric was free to return to his family at Tientsin.

The war was escalating, and Eric knew it was only a matter of time before it would be unsafe for Florence and his daughters to remain in China. Florence was expecting their third child. He arranged to send them by ship to Canada, hoping to join them soon. He took his daughter Patricia on his knee and told her through tears, "Now Tricia, I want you to look after Mummy and help her with Heather and the new baby."[74] She hugged him and promised. He whispered to Florence, "Those who love God never meet for the last time"—a saying his mother had often shared with him when parting company.[75]

Eric began writing a book to instruct Chinese pastors on how to effectively lead their churches. He spoke at church meetings. Things were growing tense in China, and he had a message of hope he felt compelled to share.

A Missionary Prisoner

In the following months, the United States and Great Britain entered World War II. Japan established **internment camps** for Westerners still living in China. Eric was now a prisoner, but he was still a missionary and never forgot that. On March 30, 1943, he entered the Weihsein internment camp hundreds of miles west of Tientsin. It was surrounded by high walls, electric fences, and searchlights, all meant to prevent escape. All 1,800 prisoners, half of whom were children, were assigned work to do. They would have to cook, hand wash their clothes, clean the toilets, and manage to get along in the overcrowded conditions. Eric became known as "Uncle Eric." He was the math teacher, coach, and chaplain for the children. He was a friend and encouraged all. Thankfully, they were able to hold church services and Bible studies.

Food and supplies were scarce, and as the months passed, Eric, who was once Scotland's athletic champion, became weak and thin. Early in 1945, Eric began to suffer from headaches. On Sunday, February 11, he suffered a small stroke. Doctors began to suspect he had a brain tumor, which was confirmed after his death. On February 21, he walked feebly to the post office and mailed this letter to Florence. "Was carrying too much responsibility. Am much better after a month in the hospital. Doctor suggests changing my work. Giving up teaching and athletics and taking up physical work like baking … a good change. Keep me in touch with the news. Enjoying comfort and parcels. Special love to you and the children."[76]

That evening, Eric was taken to the hospital again. He wrote the first words of his favorite hymn on a scrap of paper and handed it to one of the missionary nurses. It said, "Be still my soul."[77] He died peacefully in his sleep. The whole world mourned Eric's death.

The Edinburgh Evening News described him this way: "One of the best known and most admired men who ever took part in sport, whose devotion to his principles won him the highest esteem."[78] A British filmmaker was inspired by Eric's life and made a movie that won the Academy Award in 1981: *Chariots of Fire*.

Chinese Disciples

In 1949, all Christian missionary work in China effectively came to an end. Missionaries were no longer permitted into the country. However, the Christian work done by missionaries such as Eric Liddell, his parents, Hudson Taylor, and others would continue to produce fruit in the lives of the Chinese people. It is estimated that there may be close to 100 million professing Christians in China today. As Isaiah 55:11 tells us, "So shall my word be that goeth forth out of my mouth: it shall not return unto me void, but it shall accomplish that which I please, and it shall prosper in the thing whereto I sent it."

8

Betty Greene

Missionary Pilot

1650 1700 1750 1800 1850 1902–1945 2000 2050

"*Missionary Aviation Fellowship pilots are not just pilots.... We are missionaries helping other missionaries.*"[79]

Seattle, Washington – Betty and her twin brother were born in 1920. Growing up with exciting stories of planes, she dreamed of flying.

Sweetwater, Texas – After completing a program to train pilots, she signed up with the Women's Airforce Service Pilots. She also envisioned using planes for mission work.

Mexico City, Mexico – She would begin to show how planes were vital to remote areas, from South America to Africa and beyond.

Medina, Washington – Betty, with Alzheimer's, lost her memory. She died on April 10, 1997. She was an inspiring visionary of missionary flights.

Who Was Betty Greene?

From the time Betty Greene was a young woman, she had two passions in life: her love for Jesus Christ and her love of flying. She was inspired by an older woman to combine those two loves and use her skill as a pilot to serve God. She became one of the first women missionary pilots and was one of the founders of Mission Aviation Fellowship. Today, this organization owns over 80 planes that aid missionaries in 19 countries.

Early Years

Elizabeth (Betty) Greene was born in Seattle, Washington, in 1920. She and her twin brother Bill were the youngest of four children. Their parents were devoted Christians who started a Sunday school for neighborhood children. They raised their children to love and serve God.

Betty grew up hearing about the adventures of Charles Lindbergh, who flew the *Spirit of St. Louis* from New York to Paris, France. When she was eight, she had the exciting privilege of seeing him perform and deliver a speech at the University of Washington. She was there with her older brother Joe, who also loved airplanes and obtained his pilot's license when he was 14. Betty noticed Lindbergh was wearing the Distinguished Flying Cross pin he had received from President Coolidge. What an exciting day for Betty! There was nothing she wanted more than to be able to fly one day.

solo: by oneself

Her Wish Comes True

For Betty's 16th birthday, her father arranged for her to take an airplane ride. It was exhilarating! Her uncle gave her $100 as a gift, and Betty decided to use the money for flying lessons. Two weeks after the first lesson, she flew **solo**. Then her money ran out. Her mother insisted she go to college to become a nurse. Betty followed her mother's advice but hated every moment of her studies. Finally, her mother realized nursing was not a good fit for Betty.

Betty left school and began helping her father in the office. She also taught the youth group at the Presbyterian church her family attended. One day, she visited a 70-year-old family friend, Mrs. Bowman. Mrs. Bowman asked Betty what things she loved to do most of all. That was an easy answer — flying and helping with the youth group at church. Mrs. Bowman encouraged her to consider that God had given her these desires. Just maybe, He wanted her to combine both loves and use her flying skills for mission work. Betty thought that would be too good to be true. The idea was so exciting! She silently prayed on the way home, "God, I've never heard of anyone who used flying to help spread the gospel message, but if You want me to fly for You, show me how to make it happen."[80]

Pilot Training Program

The United States was preparing for the possibility of involvement in World War II. As a result, the University of Washington opened a new program for training pilots. Betty's parents encouraged her to apply. Betty was accepted in 1941, one of three women in the class of 40 people. It was a dream come true. Betty spent hours practicing landing and taking off in a **float plane**. She passed the course with exemplary grades.

Betty read an article in the newspaper about women pilots being trained for the military. Although they would not be allowed in combat, they would take on flying projects which would give the male pilots more flexibility. Incredibly, her parents had read the same article and contacted Mrs. Sheehy, the woman in charge of WASP, the Women's Airforce Service Pilots organization for **civilian** women pilots. Mrs. Sheehy met with Betty and accepted her into the program. Betty was

float plane: a seaplane supported on water by floats

civilian: non-military

soon on her way to Avenger Field in Sweetwater, Texas.

Days were spent in flying practice and instruction. Afternoons and evenings were spent studying. Betty set her mind to learn all she could about flying, intending to use her training for mission work when the war ended. She wrote an article about why she wanted to fly. It was published in *His*, an InterVarsity Christian Fellowship magazine. She did not know at the time how this article would define the direction of her life.

Camp Davis

Upon graduation, Betty and two classmates were sent to Camp Davis for duty. They later learned they were replacements for two pilots who had just been killed in flying accidents. Their assignment was to pull a large fabric banner behind their plane to provide target practice for men on the ground being trained to use anti-aircraft guns. Her first target-towing mission proved to be a scary one — some of the men on the ground were mistaken and aimed at her aircraft, not the banner. That was a close call. After several weeks, she was reassigned to Wright Field in Dayton, Ohio, to experiment with high flying altitudes. This was dangerous work, but Betty was more than happy to participate.

An Interesting Letter

In 1944, Betty received a letter from Jim Truxton. It said, "Dear Miss Greene, I read your article in last year's spring issue of *His* magazine and wanted to tell you that you are not alone. There are several other airmen who share your vision for using aircraft and pilots to spread the gospel to the ends of the earth."[81] Jim wanted to meet Betty in Washington, D.C., to discuss becoming a part of CAMF (Christian Airman's Missionary Fellowship). In July, Betty was sent to the Pentagon to meet an official from WASP. Here was her chance! She contacted Jim and arranged to meet. He wanted Betty to go to Los Angeles and set up CAMF's first office. The idea excited her, and she promised to pray about it. As much as she wanted to accept the offer, however, she decided she could not leave WASP while the war was still going on. **Providentially**, shortly after that, Betty heard WASP would be disbanded in November. She would be free to pursue CAMF!

providentially: occurring as if by divine intervention

Christian Airman's Missionary Fellowship

Dawson Trotman, an evangelist and founder of the Navigators organization, met Betty at the Los Angeles airport and invited her to stay with his family in the two-story mansion previously gifted to CAMF. The day after she arrived, Dawson drove her to the Navigators' main office in Los Angeles, where he had made an office ready for her use. Jim Truxton had asked her to produce a booklet explaining the aims of CAMF. By the end of the day, Betty had clarified eight goals for CAMF:

1. To provide Christian airmen who have been in the military with an outlet to use their skills after the war was over.
2. To provide worldwide, inexpensive missionary bases where pilots and mechanics could live and work.
3. To transport missionaries and supplies to remote places.
4. To gather information about weather patterns and safety.
5. To fly mechanics wherever they are needed.
6. To provide pilots and aircraft to assist in rescue efforts.
7. To publish a newsletter to inform the public of CAMF's work and needs.
8. To start CAMF groups in many countries.

The mission was exciting, and Betty was thrilled to be a vital part of the effort. She began writing letters to anyone she thought might help, and donations started to come in. CAMF needed one indispensable thing — an airplane. Betty published a flyer called *Speed the Light on the Wings of the Wind* to help raise money. Above all else, Betty prayed for God to bless their efforts with success.

Wycliffe Bible Translators

Wycliffe Bible Translators was an organization that translated the Bible into many languages. They had a problem, though. Some people who needed Bibles lived in areas that were so remote no roads existed. Distribution of Bibles in those places was almost impossible. They realized aircraft would be a tremendous advantage for their ministry.

Wycliffe knew about CAMF and invited Betty to fly to Mexico City to meet Cameron Townsend, the founder of Wycliffe Bible Translators. She accompanied Townsend to the remote area of El Real, a jungle training camp. She later wrote, "I lived with the missionaries there for two months and it really opened my eyes to how these translators live and work. I stayed in a tiny mud hut with another female missionary and our kitchen was a smaller mud hut. Mosquitoes were a menace, and I wasn't the only one who suffered from malaria."[82] She concluded that an **amphibious** aircraft would best meet the need, as there was more water than dry ground on which to land a plane. Betty was with Wycliffe for three and a half months before returning to Los Angeles. She was convinced there was a great need for aircraft in mission work. Wycliffe invited CAMF to work alongside them, providing the pilots and aircraft.

amphibious: adapted for land and water

biplane: aircraft with two main wings stacked one above the other

Aircraft Is Purchased

CAMF (later named MAF — Missionary Aviation Fellowship) finally located and purchased their first aircraft in February 1946, a Waco **biplane**. Betty was the first pilot on its maiden flight. She

prepared to fly 2,100 miles to Mexico City and from there to the jungle camp. March was her first full month of service out of El Real. She logged in for more than 32 hours and transported 49 passengers. By not having to journey on foot, the passengers were saved 50 weeks of **grueling** travel on rugged jungle trails.

grueling: difficult, requiring considerable effort

Soon another pilot, George Wiggins, relieved Betty so she could begin a new Wycliffe work. Wycliffe Bible Translators had purchased a Grumman Duck amphibious plane, and Betty was to fly it to the Amazon jungle in Peru. On December 20, 1946, she was the first woman to pilot an aircraft across the dangerous Andes Mountains. Even though that was a remarkable achievement, it was more significant to Betty that she had flown a plane to a remote location where missionaries desperately needed her services.

There was plenty of work for Betty to do. New Wycliffe camps were being established in the Amazon jungle. By January, Betty had completed 23 flights over the jungle. She rescued a missionary who was dangerously ill and would never have survived the tedious trek by land to the hospital. As Betty later wrote, "Missionary Aviation Fellowship pilots are not just pilots, they are missionaries too. We are missionaries helping other missionaries."[83]

Betty not only helped missionaries but also assisted the Peruvian government by flying their officials to different locations. Of course, Betty shared the gospel with them all. On one occasion, she transported the president of Peru to San Pablo. He invited Betty to come to a party he was hosting. Here she was honored for the work she had done. He presented her with two macaws — colorful parrots! It was a tradition for Peruvians to give gifts to those they appreciated. While working there, Betty was given the parrots, a baby tiger, a turtle, two baby monkeys, and a boa constrictor. Although she appreciated their kindness and loved animals, she passed the animals on to others for lack of time to care for them properly.

A New Mission Field

Betty took a three-and-a-half-year break to help her aging parents. In February 1951, Betty flew to Nigeria to relieve a missionary couple who needed a two-year furlough. She worked with the Sudan Interior Mission (SIM). After leaving Seattle, Betty flew 9,000 miles before arriving in Kano, Nigeria. She went right to work. One of her first flights was taking an expectant mother to the hospital to deliver her baby. A Nigerian storm was brewing, and they had to wait until it passed. The storm was so violent that Betty and a helper had to weigh down the Cessna aircraft with cement blocks to keep it from blowing off the runway. By daybreak, the storm had died down, and Betty flew the mother to the hospital just in time for the baby to be born. On her next mission, she encountered a **harmattan**. Her passengers were a new mother and her four-week-old baby flying home to reunite with her family. Betty prayed for guidance as the storm worsened. She finally got the plane safely to the closest airfield where they waited until the dust storm subsided two days later. Betty had many medically related flights while in Nigeria.

harmattan: a severe dust-laden wind occurring on Africa's coast

Another Mission Field

Sudan at the time was the biggest country in Africa. For much of the year, it was a dry desert, but the Nile River flooded from November until May. The floods were essential to prepare the ground for crops being planted. Much of the land was underwater for months each year. Villages were built on the high ground, but villagers were isolated from the mainland when the floods came. Missionaries and mission stations were also **impeded** from doing their work. Having airplanes to fly in necessities and transport the sick was crucial. Additionally, Betty transported missionaries' children to boarding school and home for vacation times. She flew doctors and nurses who ran clinics to remote villages. She brought people who needed complex surgeries to more modern hospitals.

Betty was an accomplished pilot. She had flown 2,239 hours without having any accidents. That changed on July 9, 1957. She was transporting a missionary family when her Cessna aircraft was caught

impeded: hindered, prevented

crosswind: a wind blowing in a direction not parallel to a course

in a **crosswind**. She managed to land, keeping the passengers safe, but the Cessna was heavily damaged. Thankfully, the broken wings were removable, and she sent them off for repair. Betty worked in Sudan for two years; then she was needed in Dutch New Guinea. Many areas of New Guinea were unexplored and unmapped. The people lived in a primitive culture.

Betty served as an MAF pilot for 16 years, flying in 12 countries, and touching down in some 20 more. In 1962, she began working at MAF headquarters. She helped train the men and women who volunteered to work with MAF. It excited her to think that an idea that started in the minds and hearts of four people had grown to serve missionaries throughout the world. She also served as prayer secretary, alerting people about prayer needs for the organization. She wrote, "As I look back over the years and realize that from one operation in Mexico in 1946, the Lord expanded the work of MAF to over 40 operations in many different countries, I give thanks to Him. How rewarding it has been to be part of such a wonderful team."[84]

When Betty was 70 years old, she began losing her memory. She was diagnosed with Alzheimer's disease. When she could no longer take care of herself, a friend from MAF moved in to help her. In early April 1997, Betty caught a cold and never fully recovered. She died on April 10.

The Mission Aviation Fellowship Betty helped found is still functioning. It operates 84 airplanes, with 47 bases in 19 countries. "It is the world's largest fleet of private aircraft. Every four minutes, seven days a week, 365 days a year, a MAF-US airplane takes off or lands somewhere in the world. Each year, these aircraft fly nearly five million miles, landing at some 3,000 different landing strips while serving over 500 Christian and humanitarian organizations."[85] God blessed the efforts of this woman whose main desire was to use her flying skills to spread the gospel of Jesus Christ to the ends of the earth.

9 Jim Elliot

Called to Give His Life

1927–1956

"*May I burn up for Thee … I seek not a long life, but a full one like yours, Lord Jesus.*"[86]

Portland, Oregon – Born in 1927 in Portland, Oregon, Jim was raised in a family with a strong Christian faith who also hosted missionaries in their home.

Chicago, Illinois – He attend Wheaton College, trusting God to meet his needs. He began to plan to become a missionary, especially in South America.

Quito, Ecuador – Jim proposed to Betty, who was also helping with the ministry. He also was translating Scripture into Quichua language.

Shandia, Ecuador – In 1956, during Operation Auca, Jim and four others were killed. Even so, their families were determined and finished the Auca mission work.

Who Was Jim Elliot?

Jim Elliot was an American Christian missionary to the Auca Indians in Ecuador. He and four other friends were killed while trying to evangelize the fierce jungle tribe. Shortly after he completed his education at Wheaton College, he wrote in his journal, "He is no fool who gives what he cannot keep to gain that which he cannot lose."[87] That is how he lived, and his testimony has inspired countless thousands to dedicate their lives to the Lord.

Early Years

chiropractor: professional who treats back and neck pain and the musculoskeletal system

chasm: separation

Jim Elliot was born on October 8, 1927, and was one of four siblings. His father was a full-time evangelist, and his mother was a **chiropractor**. Jim's parents had a strong Christian faith and took their children to church regularly. The family read the Bible daily. Obedience, honesty, and Christian character were fostered in the children. After attending a Christian service one night, six-year-old Jim told his mother, "I'm saved now."[88] From that night on, he talked about his salvation to all his friends. After explaining to his friend DK about how sin entered the world and created a **chasm** between man and God, he used an illustration of a bridge to explain salvation. "When Jesus died on a cross, it was so that those who trust in him, and ask him to forgive their sins, could have their sins forgiven. He opened the way back to God. Jesus is like a bridge that allows all who trust in Him to cross over the chasm of sin and go to heaven when they die."[89] The Elliots often opened their home to traveling missionaries, and Jim got to know many of them. Their stories made quite an impression on him.

When Jim was 14, his father told him something he never forgot. He explained how he and his mother had tried to bring their children up as Christians. When they disobeyed, they were corrected. Then he told Jim that at 14, he was a man responsible to God for his actions. "But remember this, there will have been times in the past when you got off with doing something wrong because your mother and I didn't know anything about it, but God knows everything, and He has his own way of punishing."[90]

Off to College

Jim felt strongly that he should attend Wheaton College near Chicago, Illinois, for his college education. It had a sound academic reputation and challenged its students to live a life dedicated to Jesus. It was a long way from home. Finances were tight, and he had to depend on the Lord to meet his needs. After two months, Jim wrote home, reporting that God had provided all he needed. A friend gave him a gift of money, he received a scholarship, and even found a part-time job. Jim was focused on preparing to be a missionary. He was inspired to pursue God. He disciplined himself to get up early to pray and read the Bible before starting each day. He had a strong desire to translate the Bible into languages tribal people could understand.

Jim learned that there was one Christian worker in the United States for every 500 people. In foreign lands, however, there was only one Christian worker for every 50,000 people. He was not sure where God would have him serve, except that it would be on some foreign field.

During summer break in 1947, he had the opportunity to serve a short term in Mexico. He began to study Spanish there. Jim began writing daily in a journal while he was in Mexico. This entry expressed the desire of his heart: "May I burn up for Thee. **Consume** my life, My God, for it is Thine. I seek not a long life, but a full one like yours, Lord Jesus."[91] Little did he know, he would not live a long life.

consume: deeply affect

Meeting Elizabeth

During his third year at college, Jim Elliot met Elizabeth (Betty) Howard. Her parents had been missionaries. She and Jim shared many interests, and both desired to be used by God in foreign lands. Elizabeth graduated a year before Jim, and the couple parted, hoping that they would eventually be able to marry. Elizabeth was bound for Alberta to do missionary work there. Jim spent that summer traveling with a gospel team, preaching to groups of young people at summer camps and churches.

In September 1948, Jim began his last year of college. He and Elizabeth wrote to each other often, and their love for one another grew. Early in 1949, Jim began to develop a growing passion for tribal work in the South American jungle. He received a letter from his brother Bert, a missionary in Peru. Bert told him of a missionary, Dr. Tidmarsh, who had been working for years with the **Quichua Indians,** who speak the Quichua (Spanish spelling) languages. Dr. Tidmarsh's wife had recently become very ill. The couple needed to leave the mission station he had set up in the jungle to get medical treatment for her. At **Shandia**, Dr. Tidmarsh had established a boys' school and medical clinic. Several Quichua people had become Christians. Dr. Tidmarsh asked if Bert knew anyone who could take over the mission work that he had begun. Jim felt drawn to this ministry and wondered if this was where God wanted him.

Quichua Indians: a group of indigenous peoples of South America

Shandia: village in the rainforest of eastern Ecuador

providentially: planned by God

Camp Wycliffe

That summer, Jim attended Camp Wycliffe in Oklahoma City. There, missionaries who had lived in remote areas of the world and mastered little-known languages were assigned to each student. Jim **providentially** was assigned to a retired missionary who had worked in Ecuador among the Quichua Indians. Jim's heart raced. This could not just be a coincidence. During the next few weeks, Jim learned that the Quichua population numbered over 800,000, but only 5 missionaries were working with them. The missionary told Jim of a primitive tribe of Indians called the

Aucas (a modification of *awqa*, the Quichua word for "savages"). They were an isolated tribe known for their violence and were one of the most difficult to reach. They did not like outsiders and were likely to kill them on sight. Jim began to pray that he might reach them with the gospel message.

Jim dedicated the next ten days to pray, asking God for guidance. At the end of that time, he felt sure he knew the direction to pursue. He asked God for another young man to accompany him. He decided to begin learning Quichua along with Spanish. He wrote to Dr. Tidmarsh to tell him he wanted to take over his work at Shandia. He thought of his old roommate from Wheaton, Pete Fleming, and wrote to him. "I would certainly be glad if God persuaded you to go with me.... But He must persuade you. All I can do is pray for a cleared path for you."[92] Pete had been saved at age 13, and his fellow college students had been impressed with his consistent Christian testimony. Jim's prayer for a companion was answered when Pete Fleming decided to join him.

On to Quito

On February 21, 1952, they arrived and were met by Dr. Tidmarsh at the dock at Guayaquil, Ecuador. He had tickets ready for them to fly to **Quito**. Jim and Pete planned to

Quito: capital city of Ecuador

stay with the Tidmarshes at the Gospel Missionary Union until they were more fluent in Spanish. Dr. Tidmarsh had a tutor ready to help them.

Betty visited Jim for a few months while he stayed at the Gospel Missionary Union, much to his delight. She felt God was calling her to Ecuador. She studied Spanish with Jim and Pete. They learned very quickly, motivated by the desire to be useful to the Lord. By the end of July, Jim knew enough Spanish to preach a service. At about this time, Betty moved to the foot of the Andes Mountains to help translate the Bible for the Colorada Indians. Jim and Pete moved on to Shandia, where they would be based. While walking on the trail that led to Shandia, Jim thought, "Right on time — Right on time — God's time. My joy is full — full — full!"[93] His dream was coming true at last.

Preparation Time

Jim and Pete soon began building an airstrip. Each morning, they spent time studying the language. The Quichua people soon began to trust them. Jim and Pete were encouraged when the Indians complimented them on how well they were learning the language. It seemed so slow to them at times. Dr. Tidmarsh taught them some basic medical knowledge for ministering to the tribes. Jim experimented with growing crops. The natives really had no experience with vegetables before that. Jim enjoyed teaching the boys in the school Dr. Tidmarsh had established. He also led them in team sports. Jim and Pete's friend from college, Ed McCully, along with his wife, arrived in Quito in December 1952. They enthusiastically began learning Spanish, planning to move to Shandia as part of the team.

In 1953, Jim wrote to Betty, asking her to meet him in Quito. There, he proposed to her. Betty determined to begin learning the Quichua language while waiting to get married. Her work with translation was over. She moved in with a missionary family who were fluent in Quichua. She learned quickly while attending church and Bible studies and helping them in their ministry. Jim and Betty were married on October 8, 1953, in the Quito Registry Office with the Tidmarshes and the McCullys as witnesses. After a short honeymoon, they were flown back by Nate Saint, a Missionary Aviation Pilot. They did not know at the time that the Auca team was coming together. On April 1, Jim and Betty moved into their home in Shandia.

The Team Works Together

fiancée: a woman to be married

feud: a long, bitter conflict

About a year later, a little girl was born to Jim and Betty. They named her Valerie. She was born in Nate and Marj Saint's home. Betty and Marilou McCully enjoyed time together. Marilou gave birth to her second child in 1954. Jim remained busy translating the Scriptures into the Quichua language while conducting classes for young Quichuan converts. Pete returned briefly to the United States to marry his **fiancée**, Jim had successfully built a house, an airstrip, and a base for a new school in Shandia, as well as having supplied believers there with a few Scriptures in their own language. Now he wanted to turn his energies to befriend the Aucas. His aim was to do the same for the Auca tribe as he had done in Shandia. Their only Auca contact was a woman named Dayuma, who had escaped several years previously after a tribal **feud**. She was working on an estate of a man named Don Carlos who had survived many Auca attacks. He and Dayuma both told the men to never trust the Auca. "To you, they may seem friendly for a while, but they will not stop short of killing."[94] Instead of being discouraged, the men became surer of their mission. Pete wrote in his diary, "Savage stone-age killers who have never been reached by the Gospel before need the message of God's redeeming love more than many others. I have a quiet peace about it."[95]

Jim hiked the four-hour trail to Dayuma's house to learn phrases from her to try to communicate to the Aucas that they were bearers of goodwill and came in peace. In September 1955, Nate, flying his yellow Piper plane over Auca territory, spied a cluster of Auca houses. Aware of the danger of dealing with this tribe, the five men

began a regular program of dropping gifts from the air as tokens of friendship.

Operation Auca

The wives helped their husbands prepare the gifts to drop. One of the first gifts was a new machete. The whole campaign was carefully planned. They all knew the risks. Elizabeth Elliot wrote years later, "Jim Elliot considered himself disposable."[96] Although fearful at first when the plane dropped down to low levels, the Indians came to expect it and ran to see what gifts would be sent. The plane would lower a bucket containing items such as a metal kettle with a lid, a bag of salt, or brightly colored buttons and ribbons. The Aucas would eagerly gather up the gifts. Jim would holler out phrases he had learned from Dayuma. "I like you. I am your friend."[97] Finally the Aucas began reciprocating by placing gifts in the bucket for the men, such as headbands with brightly colored feathers, a smoked monkey tail, two squirrels, and a parrot.

pragmatic: realistic, sensible

The men ultimately decided to land on the strip of beach and build a shelter. They planned to make a tree house and stock it with supplies they might need for several days. They wanted to have a face-to-face meeting with the natives. They were **pragmatic** and took guns with them in case they had to defend themselves, but they determined to use the weapons only if necessary to scare away the men, not kill them.

Tuesday, January 3, 1956, was the day set for Operation Auca. Conditions were ideal for flying. Five days earlier, Jim had written a letter to his father, saying, "… they have never had any contact with white men other than killing. They have no word for God in their language, only for the devil and spirits. I know you will pray."[98] Jim kissed Betty and Valerie and headed out. The men sang a hymn together and prayed, then took off.

Landing on the beach had risks. The men knew if the plane were damaged, they would be at the mercy of the Aucas. Nate made five trips dropping off each man; he was the last, landing the plane. Before he did, he flew over the Auca village and called out a message, "Come to the river tomorrow."[99] The men spent the first night safely in their tree house. The next day, Nate flew over the Auca settlement again and was encouraged to see a man pointing in the direction of the river, indicating they would come. Suddenly a man and two women appeared. The men spoke all their welcoming phrases and offered them presents — knives and machetes. The man whom the missionaries nicknamed George indicated he would like a ride in the plane; of course, the missionaries were excited to oblige. "George" enjoyed the ride and waved to his fellow Aucas

below as they flew over their village. Upon returning to the beach, the missionaries prepared food for the natives and ate with them.

The Final Day

The man and the women headed back through the forest. The missionaries climbed up to the tree house, in great expectation for the following day. The wives sent food each of the five days; Nate and Pete took messages back and forth by plane. Nate sent a message to Marj, who was manning the radio: "Pray for us. I believe today is the day."[100] Sunday, January 8, was going to be a day to remember! Nate promised to contact her at 4:30 with the good news of the day's encounter.

The wives waited anxiously, but that call never came. Years later, some of the Auca people told them what had happened. At about 3:00 p.m., three Auca women appeared. Jim and Pete started to meet them, but they did not appear friendly. They heard a horrible scream behind them and turned to see Auca warriors running toward them with spears. The missionaries had purposed not to kill any Auca people to save their own lives. They had come to share the gospel, not to kill. Seconds later, Nate Saint was speared. As he fell to the ground, his watch was smashed, and the hands of the watch stopped at 3:10 p.m. Ed McCully raced over to help him when a spear was thrust in his back. Roger ran toward the airplane, probably to send a message. Pete hollered in their language that they came to meet them, not hurt them. Pete was speared, and then Roger. Jim was the last to be speared, and his body fell face down in the Curaray River and floated downstream.

Johnny Kernan was an **auxiliary pilot** who sometimes worked with Nate. He flew out the next morning. He reported the plane had been stripped of its fabric, but he saw no sign of the five missionaries. By Monday night, news had reached the world. Rescue teams arrived to help search. Two bodies were found Wednesday morning. By Thursday morning, four bodies had been recovered. Ed's body was never found. The wives conveyed this message for the grief-stricken world that was watching, "The Lord has closed our hearts to grief and hysteria and filled them with His perfect peace."[101]

auxiliary pilot: volunteer pilot

The Rest of the Story

No one would have blamed the missionaries' wives for leaving immediately for safety in the United States. Yet, each wife shared the commitment of her husband to spread the gospel message. Marilou returned to the States to deliver her third child but returned to

Ecuador to work with Marj Saint at the missionary headquarters in Quito. Barbara began to work with the Jivaro tribe, a warlike South American tribe living in Ecuador. Betty, now better known to the world as Elizabeth Elliot, returned to Shandia with 10-month-old Valerie. Rachel Saint, Nate's sister, continued to learn the language with Dayuma as her teacher. Flights bearing gifts resumed over Auca territory. Elizabeth taught in the school Jim and Pete had established, did some medical work, and continued translating the Scriptures into the Quichua language. Dayuma went with Rachel Saint to the United States for a short visit and there became a Christian.

Two years later, two Auca women came to Elizabeth, who welcomed them into her home. On September 3, 1958, the two women and Dayuma returned to the Auca tribe. Three weeks later, they came back to invite Elizabeth, Valerie, and Rachel to come to live in the jungle with their tribe. The Auca people wished to hear more about the God that Dayuma had come to know. Finally, the gospel, for which the five missionaries gave their lives, was presented to the Auca tribe face to face. On October 6, 1958, Elizabeth, Valerie, and Rachel Saint went to live among the tribe. Elizabeth and Valerie stayed for two years. Rachel remained with the tribe for her entire life and helped to lead many Auca people to the Lord Jesus, including at least one of those who had taken the life of her brother and his friends. Elizabeth returned to the United States and wrote *Through the Gates of Splendor*, the story of Operation Auca. She authored over 20 books to inspire Christians to walk faithfully despite desperate circumstances. She has been an encouragement to millions of Christians through her writing and speaking, sharing the mission for which Jim willingly gave his life.

"When You were on earth, You made blind men see. Today I pray, that You will make seeing eyes blind."[102]

Sint Pancras, Holland – Andrew was born in 1928, and as he grew older, he had a habit of slipping out of church services to explore. World War II brought hardships.

Holland – He joined the Dutch Resistance. After the war, he joined the military and worked at a chocolate factory. He met Corrie, and they began sharing the gospel.

Eastern Europe – Discovering the truth in Communist countries with no access for Bibles and a growing number of refugees, Andrew began personally smuggling Bibles.

Harderwijk, Netherlands – He began Open Doors ministry focused on getting Bibles into the hands of those in China, Eastern Europe, and the Middle East. He died in 2022.

Who Was Brother Andrew?

Brother Andrew was a Dutch missionary who used his desire for adventure and his fearless nature to smuggle Bibles into Communist countries. He risked his life on countless occasions to bring the saving hope of the gospel to persecuted peoples. His ministry, Open Doors, continues today to deliver the message of salvation to oppressed people.

Early Years

evading: avoiding

escapades: adventures

Andrew van der Bijl, better known as Brother Andrew, was born in 1928 in Sint Pancras, Holland. He was the fourth of six children. Andrew was an adventurous boy, often bored with everyday life. He did not want to grow up to become a blacksmith like his father. Andrew had read of adventure in library books. He often dreamed up mischievous ways to add some fun to his life. He was also skillful at **evading** capture for his **escapades**. Every Sunday, his family would faithfully attend church. His father was hard of hearing, so the family always occupied the front row, close enough so he could clearly hear the sermon. The pew was not quite long enough for the entire family, so Andrew always offered to sit in the back pew. During the service, he would quietly slip out the back door and find ways to entertain himself. Since nearly everyone in town attended church, he was never caught. He was careful to enter the church building just before the service was over, and he listened to others' comments about the sermon. On Sunday afternoons, he joined in discussions with his father and their neighbors as they gathered to drink coffee and discuss the sermon. Andrew chimed in with carefully placed remarks, so no one ever suspected he had sneaked away.

Wartime

Germany, under the leadership of Adolph Hitler and his National Socialist party, was becoming aggressive toward neighboring countries. German troops had marched into Czechoslovakia and Poland, demanding territory. Britain and France declared war on Germany. People in Holland began to fear for their freedom. In April 1940, the Germans invaded Denmark and Norway, pretending to protect them from France and England. Holland knew it would not be long before they were in danger.

On May 10, the Germans began bombing Holland, Belgium, and Luxembourg. On May 14, the Dutch prime minister surrendered to the Germans. As Andrew lay in bed that night, he resolved that now that he was 12 years old, he would do his part to run the **Nazis** out of Holland. Here was an adventure that really mattered. The Germans forced Dutch residents to wear identity cards around their necks. Food was **rationed**. A curfew was established, **coercing** everyone to be in their home by 10:00 p.m. Worst of all, radios were banned. Radio was the only way Andrew's family and neighbors could get the truth about the war. Dutch broadcasters had relocated to London and broadcast news to Holland.

Nazis: members of Adolf Hitler's fascist party in Germany

rationed: limited and given in small portions

coercing: forcing

Although a terrible price would be paid if they were caught, Andrew's parents hid a radio in a tiny crawl space in the back of the loft where Andrew slept. Each child would take a turn crawling into the dark, cramped cubbyhole each night, listening to the radio and conveying the news to the family. The Germans began confiscating all the Dutch citizens' personal resources. Andrew's school was turned into an army barracks, and lessons were suspended. In 1943, the Nazis turned off electricity to the town. Food was desperately hard to obtain. The Germans began **conscripting** Dutch boys into their army. Andrew's older brother was safely hidden by the **Dutch Resistance**. Andrew dreamed of being able to join the Dutch Resistance.

conscripting: forced military service

Dutch Resistance: those collecting information and resisting Nazis

German Luger pistol: a military service gun

Andrew Has a Plan

Andrew came up with a plan to hopefully help the Dutch Resistance. Late one night, he sneaked into the house of a Dutch man, a traitor who served with the Germans. He stole the man's **German Luger pistol** without being caught. He took it to a Dutch

Resistance meeting the next night and was permitted to attend the **clandestine** gathering in exchange for giving them the Luger. He learned that the Resistance was helping Jewish people to escape across the English Channel to safety. He also learned how he could ruin the engines of German cars by putting sugar in their gas tanks. This he did two nights later. His mother commented on how the rationed sugar was disappearing, but there was a twinkle in her eye as she told of hearing that some of the Nazis were having car troubles. Andrew, now 14, also helped by escorting Jewish people to safe houses and delivering messages for the Resistance workers.

clandestine: secret

The War Draws to a Close

The D-Day invasion brought hope, and by August, Paris was liberated. By February, the Allies had liberated all of France. On May 1, 1945, the radio reported that Hitler was dead. Four days later, his successor ordered all Nazi troops to leave Holland. Sint Pancras was free at last!

Andrew wondered what he should do with his life. He decided to join the army. He excelled at the training. His training ended in November 1946. He went home to say goodbye to his family. He was off for Southeast Asia.

Life in the Army

Andrew was chosen to train as part of a **commando unit** in Indonesia. After completing the training, his unit was sent to reinforce a squad in which three-quarters of its soldiers had been killed. After a few weeks, the sense of excitement he had experienced began to wane. However, he did his job well and became known for his bravery as time went on. One day, when climbing up a hill ahead of his unit, he came face to face with ten heavily armed enemy soldiers. Thinking fast, he **bluffed** and hollered out, "The war is over for you. Drop your weapons. You're completely surrounded!"[103] To his great amazement, they surrendered. His fellow soldiers were **flabbergasted** when they caught up with Andrew and found him guarding ten prisoners at gunpoint. Then, on February 12, 1949, he was ambushed by the enemy and shot in the ankle.

commando unit: a group for hit-and-run raids in enemy territory

bluffed: hoped to trick

flabbergasted: astonished

Back Home

As Andrew lay in the hospital recovering, he wished he was dead rather than being a 20-year-old cripple. Bored and discouraged, he picked up the Bible his mother had sent with him and began to read. Somehow, it seemed to come alive for him, unlike his experiences as a boy in Sunday school. For the first time in his life, he could not put it down.

In May 1949, he was shipped home to Holland. After a brief time at home, the army sent Andrew to a rehabilitation program 60 miles away. One day, a young woman entered the ward and invited the men to a revival meeting. Andrew was moved by that service.

In November 1949, Andrew was released from the military. Back at home, he began attending church in earnest. One night in his bed, he surrendered his life to the Lord completely. Not long after that, while attending a church service, he committed his life to becoming a missionary.

Meeting Corrie

Andrew applied for a job at a chocolate factory while he decided what his next step would be. Here, he met Corrie van Dam, a young lady who stood out from the rest of the girls. Corrie said she felt that Jesus had sent her to the factory to be a friend to the female employees and tell them about the Lord. Suddenly, Andrew remembered where he had seen Corrie before. She was the girl who had invited the recovering soldiers to the revival meetings. He told her how the tent meetings had changed his life and that God called him to be a missionary. From that day forward, Andrew and Corrie determined to work together to share the gospel of Christ with the other factory employees. Because of their combined efforts, many of their coworkers were led to Christ.

Poland

One day, Andrew saw an advertisement for a youth festival scheduled in Warsaw, the capital city of Poland. It was Communist **propaganda**. For some reason, he felt that he must attend. He applied, stating that he was a Christian missionary in training and would love to attend to exchange ideas. He was accepted, much to his surprise. The students attending were shown the best of what Communist Poland had to offer. Every tour was carefully arranged so participants saw only positive and pleasant things. Andrew wondered what he would see if he strolled the streets apart from the tour group.

Early one morning, he slipped away. What he saw was drastically different than what he had been shown. He saw bombed-out buildings, extremely poor peasants in ragged clothing waiting in long lines for food, families living in makeshift shelters, and dirt and **despair** everywhere. He rejoined the group before he was missed, but he could not forget what he had seen. On the morning he was to leave, he sat reading his Bible, wondering how he could make a difference. A breeze blew his Bible open to Revelation 3:2, "Be watchful and strengthen the things which remain, that are ready to die." Suddenly, Andrew became convinced that God was calling him to spend the rest of his life ministering to people trapped behind the **Iron Curtain**. In 1955, not one missionary was working in Communist countries. Andrew responded by whispering, "OK, Lord. Here I am. Send me.[104] Back in Holland, invitations poured in for Andrew to speak. Everyone

propaganda: disinformation

despair: loss of all hope

Iron Curtain: the boundary dividing Western Europe and Eastern Europe

wanted to hear what it was like in a Communist country.

Czechoslovakia

On another student trip to Communist Czechoslovakia, he was again shown the most beautiful parts of the country and told how the people enjoyed religious freedom. He was shown to the headquarters of the Protestant churches in Prague, the capital city. Scholars were working on a new translation of the Bible. Andrew asked if it had been published yet, and the man working on it sadly sighed that it had not. He said, "It's been ready for many years, but…"[105] He stopped speaking when he saw the tour guide looking his way. Andrew asked if any other Bibles were available. The scholar, unsure how to answer, blurted out, "No, there are none. It is very difficult, almost impossible to find Bibles here nowadays."[106] The tour guide quickly led the group away, but Andrew had figured out the truth. The State was just pretending to give Christians freedom but did not plan to ever let the Bible be printed.

Andrew found a bookstore the next day and inquired if they had any Bibles for sale. He was told there were no Bibles because they were waiting for the new translation to be printed. Andrew left with a heavy heart. His last day in Czechoslovakia was a Sunday. He sneaked off to visit a church. He found that very few people had either a Bible or a hymn book. The ones who did held them way out at arm's length to share them with other parishioners. Andrew wished so much that he could place a Bible in each person's hand. The pastor told him that the government required sermons to be printed and approved before they could be preached. He then invited Andrew to speak, telling him that as a foreigner, he could deliver greetings from Holland and greetings from the Lord. Andrew spoke in four different churches that day before returning to the group. The tour guide was extremely upset that Andrew had been absent for so long. Andrew was told that he would never be allowed back in the country.

visas: document that allows a person to leave, stay, or enter another country

Yugoslavia

Andrew tried applying for **visas** from several Communist countries but was refused. He prayed that the Lord would open the door so he could distribute Bibles to distressed people. He spoke in many churches and wrote articles, talking about his experiences and raised money for Bibles. In 1956, because of the Hungarian revolt, thousands of people escaped Hungary and settled in refugee camps in Germany and Austria. Andrew volunteered to minister to them, supplying them with blankets, clothes, food, and medicine. He preached the gospel, and many were saved. "As Andrew watched the transformative power of God's Spirit in the camps, his heart was thankful."[107] He wondered, though, how many millions were still left behind the Iron Curtain who had never heard the gospel.

Andrew applied again for a Yugoslavian visa, and this time was approved. Excited, he called to share the good news with his friend, Mr. Whetstra. The Whetstras had been neighbors when Andrew was just a boy and always welcomed him into their home. He had often gone to Mr. Whetstra for counsel about decisions. The Whetstras had been thrilled when Andrew had committed his life to the Lord. Mr. Whetstra told him he had decided to give Andrew his car for the ministry. He said he and his wife had prayed about it for some time and concluded that Andrew needed the car worse than they did. Now, Andrew could fill the vehicle with Bibles to distribute behind the Iron Curtain.

confiscate: seize

Yugoslavian law prohibited foreigners from bringing printed materials into the country. They had border stations set up to **confiscate** any literature. When he arrived at the checkpoint, he observed that the cars ahead of him were being thoroughly searched and every piece of luggage checked. Every time he approached a checkpoint he prayed, "God, you have called me to take your message to those who have never heard. I need your help to do this. When You were on earth, You made blind men see. Today I pray, that You will make seeing eyes blind."[108] Time and again he witnessed how God miraculously seemed to blind the eyes of the guards, allowing him passage.

Andrew had many opportunities to speak in underground

churches. There were many close calls for his safety, but God was watching over him. He smuggled Bibles and tracts wherever he traveled. At one church in Yugoslavia, Andrew preached and, at the end, asked for a show of hands from people who wanted to give their lives to Jesus. The entire congregation raised their hands even though each one was aware of the tremendous risk involved. The people were sad that they did not have Bibles. Brother Andrew promised to return with Bibles.

Andrew Has a Helper

Andrew thought often of Corrie and went to find her. He rode his bike to her parents' house only to find out the family had moved to Amsterdam. He decided to drive to Amsterdam to try to locate her family. The van Dams were delighted to see Andrew again, for he had been their guest a few times when working at the chocolate factory. Corrie was home. She had just finished her nurse's training. Before leaving for Hungary, Andrew gathered up the courage to propose to her. He warned her of the kind of life she would be living and the many risks involved in distributing the Word of God. He told her she could think about it and give him an answer after he returned from Hungary.

As always, Andrew was carrying Bibles when he drove into Hungary. Thankfully, at the border crossing, the Bibles were not detected. Stopping for lunch at a clearing by the river, Andrew began cooking on his small portable stove. Suddenly, a boat roared up to him. Three soldiers emerged to inspect his car, one carrying a machine gun. Andrew tried to think of something he could do to distract them and politely offered them some lunch. They declined, and Andrew bowed his head to say grace before eating his meal.

For some reason, the soldiers discontinued the search and headed away in the boat. God had protected him again. Andrew spent ten days encouraging believers and pastors before heading back to Holland. Upon arrival, he went straight to the hospital where Corrie worked. She was ready with her answer. She was eager to get married and join Andrew in his dangerous mission.

West Berlin

A few weeks after their marriage, Andrew and Corrie set out, this time for West Berlin. In response to articles Brother Andrew had written about his experiences, many Dutch believers had sent him clothes to bring to the refugees. After the Communists took over East Berlin in 1949, millions of people fled to West Berlin. The city was surrounded by a thick wall, the Berlin Wall, which prevented anyone in East Berlin from crossing over to freedom. Arriving at a refugee camp, they **distributed** clothes and shoes. Corrie attended to the many sick people living in crowded, unhealthy conditions.

Andrew applied for a visa to enter East Germany. Here, he found the people controlled by fear. Food was terribly scarce, as the government had driven out private farmers and replaced them with **collective** farms. In Bulgaria, Brother Andrew found churches that had no Bibles at all. The Bibles he had smuggled in were received with many tears of joy. For his next trip, he went to Romania. Believers were grateful for the Bibles and thankful that other Christians were praying for their needs. They wept and hugged Brother Andrew when it came time for him to leave.

distributed: gave away

collective: a farm in a Communist country under government supervision

Soviet Union

Brother Andrew had been traveling behind the Iron Curtain for six years. Ever since he had been called to be a missionary, he had felt a desire to take the gospel to the Soviet Union and had studied to learn Russian. Corrie had three children now and could not go with him on this trip. A Dutchman named Hans volunteered to accompany him. They loaded the car with hundreds of Bibles and camping gear. They planned to arrive in Moscow, the capital city. They easily went through the border this time.

In Moscow, they attended church. After the service, they approached a lone man standing by the wall. They asked him how he was doing. He was surprised to learn they spoke German. He told them he lived in Siberia but had been born into a German family. Siberia was 2,000 miles away, and there were no Bibles there at all. The man explained that he had a dream in which he was told to travel to Moscow where he could find a Bible for his church. Smiling, Hans said, "You were told to go 2,000 miles all the way to Moscow to get a Bible, and we were told to go 2,000 miles from the other side of the world to come to Moscow and bring Bibles."[109] A secret meeting was arranged to quickly pass the 100 Bibles to a man who would see to their distribution. Brother Andrew dreamed of being able to print pocket-sized Bibles in the Russian and Ukrainian languages by the thousands, not just the hundreds. **Finances** were the only thing holding him back.

finances: money

Back in Holland

Brother Andrew began to collect quotes from various printers. The best estimate he got was three dollars per Bible if he had 5,000 printed. This meant he needed $15,000. The Dutch Bible Society agreed to fund half the amount for the project. In 1965, after Andrew spoke in a Dutch church, an American man approached him and suggested he travel to the United States. "You should come. The people in America need to know what is going on in Eastern Europe. They don't understand the real threat of communism to us all," the man told him.[110]

Soon, Andrew was on his way to America. After speaking at a large church in Los Angeles, John Sherrill, editor of *Guideposts* magazine, came to talk with him. Sherrill interviewed Brother Andrew before he left the country. The article received an overwhelming response. John Sherrill then wanted to write a book about Brother Andrew's ministry. It was called *God's Smuggler* and was published in 1967. It was instantly a best-seller. From the proceeds, Andrew finally had enough money to buy several cars, a mechanic to

work on the cars, and money to print thousands of Bibles. His dream had come true at last!

Open Doors with Brother Andrew

In 1966, Brother Andrew learned that Chinese officials were trying to dissolve any churches established in China. He prayed for funds to print Chinese Bibles and opportunities to distribute them. He met an American ex-Marine living in the Philippines who went by the name of Brother David. He also was working to find a way to get Bibles into China. Andrew hoped they could join forces.

Andrew's ministry kept growing. He opened offices in the United States, England, and Asia, along with his office in Holland. He decided to call his growing ministry "Open Doors with Brother Andrew." He chose this based on Revelation 3:8, "… I have set before you an open door, which no one is able to shut …" (ESV).

Brother Andrew met with Brother David, who assured him that the underground church in China was alive and well. He estimated that millions of Chinese people attended house churches hidden from the government. The two men planned "Operation Pearl" to smuggle one million Bibles into China in one shipment. They planned to carry Bibles by sea to a deserted beach near Swatow, 100 miles north of Hong Kong. Chinese contacts would then distribute them throughout the country. Brother Andrew began raising money to fund the project, which would cost over seven million dollars. "Operation Pearl" began on June 18, 1981. Several weeks later, all the Bibles had been successfully delivered to house churches.

By this time, some parts of Europe were becoming more favorable to allowing Bibles to enter their countries. In East Germany,

Andrew spoke to crowds of up to 4,000 people. Mikhail Gorbachev, the new leader of the Soviet Union, allowed Open Doors to donate one million Russian Bibles at the 1,000th anniversary celebration of the Russian Orthodox Church. Brother Andrew had prayed for years that Germany would be reunited as a country; his prayer was answered. In November 1989, the Berlin Wall was torn down.

oppressed: without rights or freedoms

In 1991, Brother Andrew worked in Albania, the most **oppressed** Communist country in Eastern Europe. While there, he preached to crowds of 8,000 and distributed tens of thousands of copies of the Gospel of John and 7,000 New Testaments. Andrew also worked to bring the gospel to Iranian Christians before stepping down from his role as president of Open Doors in 1995. Although he had officially retired, he kept in close contact with his organization, which, by that time, employed 350 workers around the world. He

outcast: cruelly set aside from others

traveled to encourage the church in the Middle East, visiting Arab and Lebanese pastors. He wrote several books and counseled many leaders around the world.

Corrie died in 2018, just six months before they would have celebrated their 60th wedding anniversary. Andrew's health was declining, and he died four years later at age 94. The pastor who conducted Andrew's funeral had recently asked him if he had his life to live again, would he change anything. Andrew had replied that he would "step out in faith more, speak up louder, love the **outcast** and the enemy without counting the cost."[111]

Timeline

1788–1812		
	1788	Adoniram Judson is born in Malden, Massachusetts.
	1795	Robert Moffat is born in Ormiston, Scotland.
	1799	London Missionary Society sends missionaries to South Africa.
	1804	Adoniram Judson enters Rhode Island College.
	1808	Adoniram Judson enters Andover Theological Seminary.
	1809	Robert Moffat begins to work as a gardener.
	1810	Adoniram Judson helps form American Board of Commissioners for Foreign Missions.
	1812	Adoniram Judson and Ann Hasseltine are married.
	1812	Adoniram and Ann Judson travel to India; she miscarries.

1812 – 1829

1812	First ABCFM missionaries are sent to India.
1813	Judson's first child is born.
1813	Robert Moffat moves to Cheshire England to work as a gardener.
1815	Judson's second child is born.
1816	Judson's second child dies.
1816	Robert Moffat sails as a missionary to South Africa.
1819	Mary joins Robert Moffat in South Africa, and they are married.
1821	Robert and Mary Moffat's first child is born. She later marries David Livingstone.
1824-1825	Adoniram Judson is in prison.
1824	John G. Paton is born in Scotland.
1825	Judson's daughter Maria is born.
1826	Ann Judson dies.
1827	Maria Judson dies.
1829	Robert Moffat's first converts are baptized.

1832 – 1855

1832	Hudson Taylor is born.
1834	Adoniram Judson marries Sarah Boardman.
1839-1843	The Moffats spend time in Britain.
1840	David Livingstone is sent to South Africa as a missionary.
1840	Judson completes Burmese Bible.
1849	Adoniram Judson completes Burmese-English dictionary.
1849	Hudson Taylor becomes a Christian and is called to China.
1850	Adoniram Judson dies and is buried at sea.
1851	Hudson Taylor works as doctor's assistant in Hull.
1852	Hudson Taylor begins medical training in London.
1853	Hudson Taylor leaves for China.
1854	Hudson Taylor settles in Shanghai.
1855	Hudson Taylor has his first Chinese convert.

1856 – 1865		
	1856	Hudson Taylor moves to Ning-po.
	1858	Hudson Taylor marries Maria Dyer.
	1858	John Paton is ordained, marries Mary Robson, and goes to the island of Tanna in the New Hebrides.
	1859	John and Mary Paton have a baby son, Peter. Mary and Peter die.
	1860-1861	Hudson Taylor gets ill and returns to London.
	1861	Hudson Taylor edits a new version of the Chinese New Testament.
	1862	Hudson Taylor qualifies as a member of the Royal College of Surgeons.
	1863	John Paton returns to Scotland to recruit more missionaries.
	1864	John Paton marries Margaret Whitecross.
	1865	Hudson Taylor writes *China: Its Spiritual Needs and Claims.*

1865 – 1874		
	1865	Hudson Taylor asks God for 24 missionaries to accompany him back to China.
	1866	Hudson Taylor returns to China.
	1866	John and Margaret Paton return to New Hebrides to Aniwa.
	1867	Hudson Taylor's daughter Grace dies of meningitis.
	1867	Amy Carmichael is born in Millisle, Northern Ireland.
	1869	John Paton holds his first communion on Aniwa.
	1870	Maria Taylor dies at age 33.
	1870	John and Margaret's son Frank is born.
	1870	Robert and Mary Moffat return to Britain.
	1871	Mary Moffat dies.
	1871	Hudson Taylor returns to England and marries Jennie Faulding.
	1872	Hudson Taylor returns to China with Jennie.
	1874	Hudson Taylor injures his back, returns to England.

1874 – 1902

1874	Amy Carmichael's father dies.
1881	Africa became a focus of Christian missions.
1883	Robert Moffat dies.
1884	John Paton goes to Great Britain to raise money for New Hebrides.
1887	Amy Carmichael moves to Belfast, accepts Christ.
1892	Amy Carmichael moves to Manchester, England, and does mission work.
1895	Amy Carmichael travels to Japan as a missionary.
1896	Amy Carmichael leaves Japan for health reasons.
1899	First Aniwa New Testament is printed.
1901-1902	Amy Carmichael establishes "Welcome Hall" in Belfast.
1902	Gladys Aylward is born.
1902	Eric Liddell is born.

1903 – 1924

1903	Amy Carmichael creates Dohnavur Fellowship in India.
1904	Jennie Taylor dies of cancer.
1905	Hudson Taylor dies.
1905	Margaret Paton dies at age 82.
1907	John Paton dies at age 82.
1911	Chinese Revolution.
1912	Amy Carmichael adopts Preena.
1914	World War I begins.
1918	World War I ends.
1920	Betty Greene is born in Seattle, Washington.
1920s	Eric Liddell becomes an international rugby player and athlete.
1923	Eric Liddell gives his testimony for first time.
1924	Eric Liddell broke records during the Olympic trials, earned a place on the British Olympic team.

1925 – 1937

1925	Eric Liddell begins teaching at Chinese College, working for London Missionary Society.
1927	Jim Elliot is born on October 8 in Portland, Oregon.
1928	Andrew van der Bijl is born on May 11.
1928	Gladys Aylward is rejected by China Inland Mission.
1928	Amy Carmichael becomes an invalid after a fall.
1929	Mission work focused on medical aid was advancing.
1932	Gladys Aylward leaves for China.
1932	Amelia Earhart is first woman to fly solo across the Atlantic.
1932	Eric Liddell ordained by Scottish Congregational Church.
1934	Eric Liddell marries Florence MacKenzie in Tientsin.
1936	Gladys Aylward becomes a Chinese citizen.
1937	Japan invades China.

1937 – 1945

1937	Eric Liddell is transferred to Church-based ministry in Siaochang, North China.
1938	The Japanese bomb Yancheng.
1938	Gladys Aylward brings 100 children safely over the mountains.
1939	World War II begins.
1940	Gladys Aylward is wounded by Japanese soldiers.
1941	Missionaries and children are held in internment camps in Weihsien, China.
1941	Eric Liddell sends wife and two children to Canada for safety. A third daughter is born.
1943	Betty Greene receives wings and joins Women Air Force Service Pilots.
1945	World War II ends.
1945	Eric Liddell dies of brain tumor in Weihsien Internment Camp.

1946 – 1951

1946	Betty Greene makes first official MAF flight, transporting two Wycliffe workers from Los Angeles to Mexico.
1946	Jim Elliot attends Wheaton College.
1946	Brother Andrew joins the Dutch Army.
1946	Jim Elliot goes on mission trip to Mexico.
1947	Gladys Aylward returns to England for surgery.
1949	China becomes Communist.
1949	Brother Andrew is shot while in army and returns to Holland. He attends a revival service.
1950	Jim Elliot hears of Auca Indians.
1950	Brother Andrew becomes a Christian and surrenders his life to become a missionary.
1951	Betty Greene begins flying in Nigeria.
1951	Amy Carmichael dies at age 83 in India.

1952 – 1958		
	1952	Jim Elliot and Pete Fleming arrive in Ecuador.
	1953	Jim Elliot marries Elizabeth Howard.
	1953	Gladys Aylward founds an orphanage in Taiwan.
	1953	Brother Andrew goes to WEC in London to train as a missionary.
	1955	Nate Saint and Ed McCully fly over Auca village for the first time.
	1955	Valerie Elliot is born.
	1955	Brother Andrew graduates WEC and travels to Poland, Czechoslovakia, Yugoslavia, and Hungary, smuggling Bibles.
	1956	Betty Greene begins flying in the Sudan at Palm Beach.
	1956	Jim Elliott and his missionary colleagues set up camp.
	1956	Elliott and the others were killed.
	1958	Dayuma, an Auca woman, returns to her tribe to share her Christian faith.

1958 – 1962

1958	Elizabeth Elliot and Valerie go to live among the Aucas.
1958	Brother Andrew and Corrie are married and work in refugee camps in West Germany and Austria.
1959	Brother Andrew visits Bulgaria and Romania; his first son is born.
1959	Brother Andrew distributes tracts throughout Europe, encouraging pastors.
1960	Betty Greene moves to Dutch New Guinea.
1960	Brother Andrew's second son is born.
1960	Brother Andrew takes a guided tour of Communist Russia.
1961	Brother Andrew's third son is born; Andrew travels to Russia and Ukraine. He sees his first pocket Bible.
1961	The Berlin Wall is erected.
1962	Betty Greene retires from field work to work in MAF headquarters.

1963 – 1989		
	1963	Brother Andrew's daughter is born.
	1964	First Russian pocket Bibles are printed and 650 distributed in Russia.
	1965	Brother Andrew travels to China and Cuba.
	1967	Brother Andrew's team grows. He publishes his book *God's Smuggler.*
	1967	Brother Andrew's ministry group, Open Doors, expands to reach millions living in Communist countries.
	1970	Gladys Aylward dies.
	1970	Eric Liddell's biography is written.
	1981	Brother Andrew's Operation Pearl delivers one million Bibles to China.
	1981	Eric Liddell's story made into a movie, *Chariots of Fire.*
	1989	Brother Andrew delivers the one millionth Bible to Russia.

1992 – 2022		
	1992	Brother Andrew launches Project Samuel — Chinese Study Bible.
	1997	Betty Greene dies in Seattle, Washington.
	1997	Brother Andrew is awarded Religious Liberty Award from World Evangelical Fellowship.
	2008	Open Doors ministers to Chinese Christians during the Olympics.
	2008	Eric Liddell voted most popular Scottish athlete.
	2012	Open Doors Volunteer Summit occurs.
	2018	Corrie Andrews dies after 59 years of marriage to Brother Andrew.
	2022	Brother Andrew dies on September 27 at age 94.

Glossary

abstinence: refraining from strong drink

affluent: wealthy

alma mater: university attended

amphibious: adapted for land and water

apprenticed: learned a trade

arduous: very difficult

auxiliary pilot: volunteer pilot

bandy: a springless cart pulled by two bulls

banyan: a large fig

becalmed: at a standstill for lack of wind

biplane: aircraft with two main wings stacked one above the other

bluffed: hoped to trick

bound for: sailing to

British Consulate: offices of British government in foreign nations

chasm: separation

chiropractor: professional who treats back and neck pain and the musculoskeletal system

cholera: an acute diarrheal infection

civilian: non-military

clandestine: secret

coercing: forcing

collective: a farm in a Communist country under government supervision

commando unit: a group for hit-and-run raids in enemy territory

commissioned: chosen for a specific task

competent: having adequate abilities

compound: buildings in an enclosed area; combine or mix

conscripting: forced military service

consume: deeply affect

contraband: illegal items

crosswind: a wind blowing in a direction not parallel to a course

cumbersome: difficult to move

dengue fever: a mosquito-born viral infection with flu-like symptoms and fever ranging from mild to severe

despair: loss of all hope

dialect: a region's specific language

dilapidated: neglected, run-down

disconsolate: dejected, downcast

dismay: disappointment, fear

dispensary: a place medicines are prepared

distributed: gave away

doctrine: beliefs taught in the Bible

drudgery: hard, unpleasant work

drunkards: people addicted to strong drink

Dutch Resistance: those collecting information and resisting Nazis

eminent: most respected and admired

en route: on the way

entailed: included

escapades: adventures

ethnicity: common cultural traditions and ancestry

evacuate: leave the town

evading: avoiding

evangelistic: presentation of the Savior

evangelizing: sharing the gospel

excelled: did extremely well

excellency: a title of high status

feud: a long, bitter conflict

fiancée: a woman to be married

finances: money

flabbergasted: astonished

float plane: a seaplane supported on water by floats

footbinding: tightly wrapping the feet of young girls

fraught: full; stressful; uneasy

freshman: first-year student

frugally: inexpensively

furlough: a time period of rest

German Luger pistol: a military service gun

grueling: difficult, requiring considerable effort

harmattan: a severe dust-laden wind occurring on Africa's coast

idolatrous: worship of false gods

impeded: hindered, prevented

impetus: driving force

internment camps: a camp for civilians during war, especially those with ties to an enemy

Iron Curtain: the boundary dividing Western Europe and Eastern Europe

joiner's: making wooden windows and doors

kraal: houses surrounding a livestock pen

labored: worked hard

leisurely: slow

lobbying: trying to influence

machinist: person using tools

malignant fever: probably yellow fever

Mandarin: a high public official who ruled mountainous villages; official language of China

martyrs: those who died for the faith

missionary: one sent to spread the gospel overseas

monopoly: exclusive control

muleteers: person who drives mules

Namaqualand: a South African desert

Nazis: members of Adolf Hitler's fascist party in Germany

occupation: enemy military's seizure of the land

oppressed: without rights or freedoms

outcast: cruelly set aside from others

pharmacist: a dispenser of prescriptions

plight: bad situation

pondered: thought about

porters: people who carry others' cargo

pounds: standard unit of money used in England

pragmatic: realistic, sensible

prayer warrior: especially skilled in prayer

predominantly: mostly

pressed on: forced themselves to continue

procure: to secure

propaganda: disinformation

providentially: occurring as if by divine intervention; planned by God

Quichua Indians: a group of indigenous peoples of South America

Quito: capital city of Ecuador

rationed: limited and given in small portions

ravaged: destroyed

reap: benefit from

reimbursed: paid back

salary: pay for work done

sanctuary: place of rest

scoffed: ridiculed scornfully

seminary: school to train pastors

shafts: long pieces of wood that normally hitch to a horse

Shandia: village in the rainforest of eastern Ecuador

shillings: British money

slums: dirty, overcrowded streets inhabited by poor people

solo: by oneself

sophomore: second-year student

sprinter: athlete who runs short distances

superstition: a fear-driven false belief

Tamil: an official language of India

traitor: one who betrays his country

translating: changing one language into another

trudged: walking though exhausted

tuberculosis: a lung disease

tutelage: instruction

undeterred: persevering through setbacks

unique: unusual, special

unscrupulous: lacking morals

valedictorian: highest achiever

viceroy: ruler in charge

visas: document that allows a person to leave, stay, or enter another country

vocabulary: words used in communication

wane: weaken

war zone: area of dangerous conflict

zayat: a Burmese building

Corresponding Curriculum

Legends of Faith Series

Missionaries for Christ • **Book 3**

All the stories in this book can correspond with the following Master Books Curriculum:

- *Language Lessons for a Living Education*
- *Elementary World Geography & Cultures*
- *Elementary U.S. Geography & Social Studies*
- *America's Story* (Series)
- *A Child's Geography* (Series)
- *The World's Story* (Series)
- *Stobaugh's American and World History* (Series)
- *History of Religious Liberty*

Endnotes

1 Janet and Geoff Benge, Adoniram Judson: Bound for Burma (Seattle, WA: YWAM Publishing, 2002).

2 Ibid, 148.

3 Irene Howat, *Adoniram Judson: Danger on the Streets of Gold* (Scotland, UK: Christian Focus Publications, 2001), 73.

4 Benge, *Adoniram Judson: Bound for Burma,* 202.

5 Ibid., 228.

6 Irene Howat, *Robert Moffat — Africa's Brave Heart* (Scotland, UK: Christian Focus Publications, 2014), 111.

7 J.C. Western-Holt, *Robert Moffat* (Grand Rapids, MI: Zondervan Publishing, 1955), 22.

8 Ibid., 29.

9 Ibid., 30.

10 Howat, *Robert Moffat — Africa's Brave Heart,* 67.

11 Ibid., 76.

12 Ibid., 87.

13 Ibid., 87.

14 Ibid., 111.

15 Ibid., 123.

16 Ibid., 164.

17 Western-Holt, *Robert Moffat,* 94.

18 Iris Clinton, *Friend of the Chiefs: The Story of Robert Moffat* (Fort Washington, PA: Christian Literature Crusade, 1973), 94.

19 Western-Holt, *Robert Moffat,* 64.

20 Margaret Kabell, *The Prophet of the Pacific: The Story of John Paton* (Cambridge, UK: Lutterworth Press, 1969), 95.

21 John Paton, *John G. Paton: Missionary to the New Hebrides: An Autobiography,* ed. Rev. James Paton (Geanies House: Christian Focus Publications, Ltd., 2009), 101.

22 Bessie L. Byrum, *John G. Paton: Hero of the South Seas* (Anderson, IN: Gospel Trumpet Company, 1924), 10.

23 John Paton, *Thirty Years with South Sea Cannibals: Autobiography of John G. Paton* (Chicago, IL: Moody Press, 1964), 21.

24 Byrum, *John G. Paton: Hero of the South Seas,* 24.

25 Kay Walsh, *John G. Paton: South Sea Island Rescue* (Scotland, UK: Christian Focus Ministries, 2002), 37.

26 Byrum, *John G. Paton: Hero of the South Seas,* 25.

27 Ibid., 46.

28 Ibid., 47.

29 Ibid., 36–37.

30 Ibid., 46.

31 Walsh, *John G. Paton: South Sea Island Rescue,* 64.

32 Byrum, *John G. Paton: Hero of the South Seas,* 76.

33 Margaret Kabell, *The Prophet of the Pacific: The Story of John Paton,* 63.

34 Ibid., 71.

35 Ibid., 73.

36 Ibid., 95.

37 Janet and Geoff Benge, *Hudson Taylor — Deep in the Heart of China* (Seattle, WA: YWAM Publishing, 1998), 23.

38 Ibid, 23

39 Ibid., 67.

40 Ibid., 72.

41 Catherine Mackenzie, *Hudson Taylor: An Adventure Begins* (Scotland, UK: Christian Focus Publications, 1999), 101.

42 A.J. Lavanderos, *Who Is Missionary Hudson Taylor?* (Synergy Solutions, 2023), 23.

43 Benge, *Hudson Taylor — Deep in the Heart of China*, 154.

44 Mackenzie, *Hudson Taylor: An Adventure Begins*, 142.

45 Benge, *Hudson Taylor — Deep in the Heart of China*, 203.

46 A.J. Broomhall, *Hudson Taylor and China's Open Century, Book Two: Over the Treaty Wall* (London: Hodder and Stoughton and Overseas Missionary Fellowship, 1982), 6.

47 Kay Walsh, *Amy Carmichael: Rescuer by Night* (Scotland, UK: Christian Focus Publications, 2004), 142..

48 Janet and Geoff Benge, *Amy Carmichael: Rescuer of Precious Gems* (Seattle, WA: YWAM Publishing, 1998), 34.

49 Kay Walsh, *Amy Carmichael: Rescuer by Night*, 77.

50 Benge, *Amy Carmichael: Rescuer of Precious Gems*, 153.

51 Walsh, *Amy Carmichael: Rescuer by Night*, 142.

52 Ibid., 142.

53 Ibid., 148.

54 Janet and Geoff Benge, *Gladys Aylward: The Adventure of a Lifetime*, 42.

55 Benge, *Gladys Aylward: The Adventure of a Lifetime*, 24.

56 Ibid., 42.

57 Ibid., 88–89.

58 Myrna Grant, *Gladys Aylward: No Mountain Too High* (Scotland, UK: Christian Focus Publications, 2003), 35.

59 Benge, *Gladys Aylward: The Adventure of a Lifetime*, 113.

60 Grant, *Gladys Aylward: No Mountain Too High*, 51.

61 Benge, *Gladys Aylward: The Adventure of a Lifetime*, 153.

62 Grant, *Gladys Aylward: No Mountain Too High*, 128.

63 Janet and Geoff Benge, *Eric Liddell: Something Greater Than Gold* (Seattle, WA: YWAM Publishing, 1998), 69..

64 Ellen Caughey, *Eric Liddell: Gold Medal Missionary* (Uhrichsville, OH: Barbour Publishing, 2000), 32.

65 Benge, *Eric Liddell: Something Greater Than Gold*, 23.

66 Ibid., 44.

67 Ibid., 45.

68 Caughey, *Eric Liddell: Gold Medal Missionary*, 138.

69 Ibid., 148.

70 Ibid., 152.

71 Benge, *Eric Liddell: Something Greater Than Gold*, 69.

72 John W. Keddie, *Eric Liddell: Finish the Race* (Scotland, UK: Christian Focus Publications, 2011), 77.

73 Caughey, *Eric Liddell: Gold Medal Missionary*, 181.

74 Benge, *Eric Liddell: Something Greater Than Gold,* 162.

75 Ibid., 184.

76 Keddie, *Eric Liddell: Finish the Race,* 131.

77 Caughey, *Eric Liddell: Gold Medal Missionary,* 188.

78 Benge, *Eric Liddell: Something Greater Than Gold,* 196.

79 Howat, *Betty Greene — Courage Has Wings* (Scotland, UK: Christian Focus Publications, 2017), 102.

80 Janet and Geoff Benge, *Betty Greene — Wings to Serve* (Seattle, WA: YWAM Publishing, 1999), 31.

81 Irene Howat, *Betty Greene — Courage Has Wings,* 49.

82 Ibid., 71.

83 Ibid., 102.

84 Ibid., 158.

85 Benge, *Betty Greene — Wings to Serve,* 192.

86 Howat, *Jim Elliot: He is No Fool,* 42

87 Irene Howat, *Jim Elliot: He Is No Fool* (Scotland, UK: Christian Focus Publications, 2005), 106.

88 Kathleen White, *Jim Elliot* (Minneapolis, MN: Bethany House Publishing, 1990), 11.

89 Howat, *Jim Elliot: He Is No Fool,* 15.

90 Ibid., 42.

91 White, *Jim Elliot,* 32.

92 Ibid., 59.

93 Ibid., 123.

94 Ibid., 101.

95 Ibid.

96 Ibid., 106.

97 Ibid.

98 Ibid., 110.

99 Ibid., 111.

100 Ibid., 117.

101 Howat, *Jim Elliot: He Is No Fool,* 150.

102 Nancy Drummond, *Brother Andrew: Behind Enemy Lines* (Scotland, UK: Christian Focus Publications, 2014), 88..

103 Janet and Geoff Benge, *Brother Andrew: God's Secret Agent* (Seattle, WA: YWAM Publishing, 2005), 65.

104 Drummond, *Brother Andrew: Behind Enemy Lines,* 72.

105 Eva Wonka, *Brother Andrew: Smuggling Bibles Behind the Iron Curtain* (Campinas-São Paulo, Brazil: Eva Wonka Books, 2024), 18.

106 Ibid., 18.

107 Drummond, *Brother Andrew: Behind Enemy Lines,* 84.

108 Ibid., 88.

109 Wonka, *Brother Andrew: Smuggling Bibles Behind the Iron Curtain,* 63–64.

110 Benge, *Brother Andrew: God's Secret Agent,* 200.

111 Ibid., 215.

The *Legends of Faith* series brings the powerful stories of Christian heroes to life for middle and high school students! Marilyn Boyer's newest series includes engaging biographies, vibrant illustrations, and timeless truths that inspire courage and faith.